# SERMONS BY THE DEVIL OF TODAY IN HELL'S PALACE OF SIN BEFORE DEATH

Published by Curious Publications
697 Third Ave. #358
New York, NY 10017
curiouspublications.com

Copyright © 2025

ISBN-13: 979-8-9914395-3-4

*Sermons by the Devil* by Rev. W. S. Harris. Originally published by the Minter
Company, 1904.
*The Devil of To-Day: His Play Between the False and The Good: Being A Searching Allegory
on The Subtle Intrigues of The Devil Within The Church, The Home, And Modern Society*
by Rev. I. Mench Chambers A. M., 1906.
*Hell Before Death* by Rev. W. S. Harris. Originally published by Luther Minter, 1908.
*The Devil's Doings: His Work in The Home, Business, Politics, Society, And Every Walk of
Life, Being Messages from The Underworld of Sin and How They Are Answered* by
Lilian M. Heath. Originally published by W. R. Vansant, 1905.
*Palaces of Sin or The Devil in Society* by Col. Dick Maple. Originally published by
National Book Concern, 1902.
*The Sight of Hell* by Rev. John Furniss. Originally published by James Duffy &
Co., Ltd., 1874.

Printed and bound in the United States of America.

# A NOTE ON THE TEXT

At the turn of the century, various Christian organizations published a collection of books warning against the temptations of Satan in modern society. Within these pages, Curious Publications has resurrected many of these lessons, offering a window into yesteryear and, if desired, allowing you to discover what you've been doing wrong and how to live more righteously.

This series of excerpts and illustrations is pulled from the following books:

- *Sermons by the Devil* by Rev. W. S. Harris (1904)
- *The Devil of To-Day: His Play Between the False and The Good: Being A Searching Allegory on The Subtle Intrigues of The Devil Within The Church, The Home, And Modern Society* by Rev. I. Mench Chambers A. M., (1906)
- *Hell Before Death* by Rev. W. S. Harris (1908)
- *The Devil's Doings: His Work in The Home, Business, Politics, Society, And Every Walk of Life, Being Messages from The Underworld of Sin and How They Are Answered* by Lilian M. Heath (1905)
- *Palaces of Sin or The Devil in Society* by Col. Dick Maple (1902)
- *The Sight of Hell* by Rev. John Furniss (1874)

Now go forth into the past, beware of the devil in disguise, and live a life well lived.

*"Get thee behind me, thou Evil One."*

# Sermons By the Devil of Today in Hell's Palace of Sin Before Death

A COLLECTION OF TURN-OF-THE-CENTURY MORALITY
LESSONS AND WARNINGS AGAINST SATAN

Curious
PUBLICATIONS

New York

# CONTENTS

*Small sins grow like small serpents, and if not conquered,*
*will take their victims down to death.*

# INTRODUCTORY HOMILY

———————— ◆◆◆ ————————

## A SERPENT SERMON BY SATAN
*Sermons by the Devil*

PREACHED along the pathway of life to those who give heed.

Along the pathway of life there are scattered a large number of beautiful buildings with costly furnishings. These are supplied with little pet snakes of sin, which can be had, free of charge, by all who are willing to accept them.

Certain snakes are kept on exhibition, and as they lie in their beautiful glass cases, they present a handsome appearance. They have neat ribbon bows tied around their necks, and certain sides of the boxes are lined with satin. In front of one of these buildings I heard a man calling out:

"Come this way! come this way! all ye who hear my voice. We have on exhibition some beautiful bosom pets. If you take one now, while it is young and small, you can train it to your liking, and I will assure you that you will not only have a novel pet, but that you will be safe from its poison forever."

A certain young man, who was passing near by, was attracted to the place, and with suspicion, he glanced at the curious little pets.

"Are these not deadly snakes that you offer?"

"Ha! ha!" laughed the Evil One, "that is what some people call them, but I assure you that you need not fear them. If you take to your bosom one of these beautiful so-called deadly pets, you will not only be free from danger but it will give new warmth to your heart as you hold it there."

"I don't like the appearance of the pets," commented the young man.

"Perhaps the appearance of some may shock you a little at first, but if you will look over the whole assortment, you will find one that will suit your fancy altogether."

Then the wicked fiend spoke very fluently about the effect that these little charmers had on the present life. His words were making a favorable impression on the young man, who considered himself proof against all forms of temptation. Strange to say, the very snake that had impressed him so horribly a short time before, now fascinated him altogether. He stood as if charmed by the little serpent that the black agent held coiled in his hand.

"This is my choice," said the young man who willingly agreed to pay the price, which was noth ing more than his promise to give it a place above his heart.

The young man carried the little serpent in his breast and allowed it to feed upon his heart's blood. The snake grew so slowly that the owner did not realize with what increasing danger it was sapping his life's energies. He was unconsciously nursing an enemy, and thereby inviting his own ruin and death. The serpent had now grown large enough that it could playfully wrap itself around the arm or waist of the young man.

In the course of time the foolish young man saw very clearly that if he would not conquer the serpent that the serpent would conquer him. So he resolved to shake the serpent off or kill it in the attempt. He never realized until then how it had fastened itself upon his very vitals, and that he was powerless in his own strength to overcome the enemy. A long and terrible battle was fought. The serpent swung itself mightily in thegreat battleand the young man, in desperation, seized it and tried to crush it with his hands or stamp it with his feet. The serpent was more than a match for the youth, who called out mightily for help, and in response to his pleadings a good angel came to him and said:

"Let Christ into your heart and he will destroy the deadly serpent of sin and will make you free again."

To these welcome words the young man gave heed and was almost persuaded to accept Christ when Satan, robed like an angel, stole to his side and whispered:

"Don't be foolish, young man. You must not expect to find help from some outside power, you are fully able to help yourself. Since you are blessed with a strong mind of your own, why go begging like a little child for help? Is it not more honorable to die like a hero fighting your own battle, than to be a weakling or a coward?"

"But I will be forever lost, if I don't get rid of this sin. I cannot conquer it myself, for I have already spent all my energy in trying to do so."

Then Satan tempted him another way by appealing to his pride, and after that by trying to frighten him. But all these proved futile, and the young man turned to the better angel and to Christ who is able to deliver. His repentance and confession brought down the power that destroyed the serpent, and the young man rejoiced greatly in his freedom.

# 1
## Leisure & Entertainment

## The Death of a Saloon-Keeper
*Sermons by the Devil*

NOTE: The following incident is taken from actual life. It is no imaginary sketch or fanciful picture. The author is not sure whether it was a case of delirium tremens or not.

SATAN appeared to a saloon-keeper who was lying in great stress upon his deathbed, and spoke to him as follows:

"Let me give you one more sermon, old fellow, before you reach your reward. You have done a noble service. You have served me well, and surely I will not forsake you in this hour of death. You need not become frightened at my presence. Come! come! stop your agitations," continued the Devil, "you need not be alarmed."

"Oh horrors! oh horrors!" shrieked the poor man, "would to God that I could have a new lease of life! How can I go out into this darkness alone?"

"I will be with you to hold your hand, and lead you to your reward," assured the Devil.

Then the poor wretch tried to concentrate his thoughts on noble things, but his sins arose before him like mountains, and he could review their terrors before his eyes.

"O! what shall I do with my sins; my awful sins; my many, many sins?" he groaned aloud.

"Trouble yourself not, forget about them and be at peace," came the voice of Satan, whose real form was now gradually unfolding itself to the dying man, at which the saloon-keeper shrank back upon his pillow and lifted his bony fingers in terror.

"Keep back! keep back! come no nearer," continued his heart-breaking appeals. Satan and his imps continued to advance and they all tried to look as beautiful as possible. But they could no longer mask themselves. The struggling man tried to find rest by fastening his eyes elsewhere. But the terrible visage of Satan was so appalling, that he could not take his eyes therefrom.

Death drew still nearer and the struggle of the unfortunate man became more intense. He made one last effort to seek refuge somewhere, but just at that moment, each one of the little company of imps presented his claim. This so distracted the mind of the man that his actions were similar to a raving maniac.

"I claim your love," demanded the first imp.

"And I claim your time," demanded another, whose grinning countenance was most terrible to behold.

"I demand your attention," spoke a third in a tone most grinding and severe.

"I demand your talents throughout all eternity," spoke the most horrible imp of all the company.

"And I demand your sacrifices to be given willingly in the kingdom to come," cried out another.

And still another in mockery said: "I demand your service," but before the imp had finished his words, Satan himself cried out, "I demand your soul, your life, your all." At this saying the imps formed a cordon around the bed, and the miserable man crouched anew at their uncanny movements.

He had been sick for many weeks and refused nearly all food. He had so fallen away in flesh that scarcely anything but skin lay over his bones. His eyes were sunken and he presented an awful appearance as he was struggling in a terrible effort to escape from the cordon of imps.

He sprang back against the head-board of the bed, lifting his bony fingers like claws, as he screamed out: "Take them away! take them away!" His cries were so horrible that no one could remain in the room with him, even his wife was compelled to leave and not one of his old chums could stand so terrible a picture of death. Some one hastened to the home of a minister in the mid-night hour, and urged him to come up at once to the hotel, and pray with the dying man. The minister hastily dressed and with Bible in hand, soon entered the hotel and noticed the terror-stricken people all around, who begged him to go into the next room and do what he could for the poor man. The situation tested the courage of the minister, for as he approached the room, he heard the unearthly shrieks of the dying man, and upon opening the door, found that all had deserted the room. He prayed for courage, and thus strengthened he walked with a steady tread up to the bedside of the man, and opened his Bible before him. Suddenly there was a calm, and for the first time in many hours, the poor wretch sank down upon his pillow in quietness.

At this sudden turn, some ventured into the room and all stood as still as death, and the dying man lay motionless, as the minister read from the word of God and spoke to him. It seemed that even the devils dared not advance farther while the Word of God was being uttered in their hearing.

The minister, after a long conference, found that nothing more could be done and was compelled to go. After he had left the room, the same terrible scenes followed. The poor wretch continuously cried out in anguish and in the pathos of appealing: "Take them away! keep them back!" No one could check the march of the very devils that were advancing to claim their own, and not being able to remain in the room they all forsook him again.

All this terrible tragedy continued until the poor body of the dying man left go of its spirit, which seemed to satisfy this pack of demons, like a piece of flesh quiets a pack of pursuing wolves.

IF A PERSON is prepared to meet death he can pass out of this life in mighty triumph, but what can be more terrible than the death of the wicked? To such death comes in its worst features. Some may not die with shrieks of terror on their lips, but their inward pangs cannot be described. The picture on the opposite page does not exaggerate the horrible experiences of some who have rejected God through life. The Evil Spirits can be seen best when the curtain of mortality is falling. The only way to a happy death is by a righteous life.

*"The saloon-keeper shrank back upon his pillow and lifted his bony fingers in terror. Satan and his imps continued to advance, and they all tried to look as beautiful as possible."*

## The Saloon Devil and Uncle Sam
*Sermons by the Devil*

ONCE upon a time the Saloon Devil looked up into the face of Uncle Sam and asked for employment.

"What kind of work do you want?" said Uncle Sam as he bent his tall form to catch the answer of the low Devil.

"To create and satisfy the appetite for strong drink."

"Very well," answered Uncle Sam, "you may go to work at once in any manner you choose."

So the Saloon Devil went to work with a high hand. He sold to the rising generation and those of riper years all manner of intoxicating beverages. The result of his work was very disastrous. He made such things as ruined souls, broken hearts, broken homes and all manner of woe, want, wretchedness and death, to say nothing of the almshouses, asylums and penitentiaries that he helped to fill.

Now it happened that Uncle Sam noticed the nature of the work done by this Saloon Devil, in turn well knew that Uncle Sam was watching him, but the Devil did not know how to cover his evil work. Sometime afterward the two met again and the following conversation took place:

"You remember, Mr. Saloon Devil, that I gave you permission to do a certain kind of work, but I never dreamed that your work would be so horrible. Now be honest and tell me what you have accomplished."

"I admit," confessed the Saloon Devil, "that my work is looked upon as being disrespectable, and I pray that you will this day make me appear more decent in the eyes of the public. By reason of your great strength and influence you have the power to place upon me a new robe of respectability."

"And how can I do that?" asked Uncle Sam in a friendly manner.

"You can adopt license laws to regulate the liquor business, and by complying with these laws, I can do an honorable business under the sanction and authority of my great Uncle Sam."

"But that will be putting my approval upon it," said Uncle Sam suspiciously.

"You can easily do that with profit to yourself by charging me a nice sum for the license. The money you get through the granting of licenses alone will be more than sufficient to run the public schools, so if there is a little harm done by the business on one side, there will be untold blessings poured out upon your children on the other side."

Uncle Sam chuckled in an odd fashion as this ingenious scheme was unfolded to him. "You are indeed a clever old Devil, and I have a mind to comply with your request. If you pay the amount of money I fix, I will protect you in your business by making it legal. Then if anyone forcibly interferes with you, I will fight him off, even if I must use the whole army and navy of the United States to accomplish it."

The Saloon Devil was highly elated over his fortunate deal. He knew that he could not live long under natural freedom unless he won some kind of public endorsement. He was perfectly willing to pay any price that Uncle Sam might demand, knowing that he could produce a cheaper grade of liquor or sell it at a higher figure, or in some way conduct the business, so that the extra cost of license would fall upon the consumers instead of the saloon-keepers.

A short time after this, one could see the powerful hand of Uncle Sam placed in protection over the Saloon Devil, and the people stood wondering at the situation.

The Saloon Devil, although robed in a respectable garment, continued to do the same horrible and dirty work as before. It seemed that nothing satisfied his greed but the most terrible outrages resulting from the use and abuse of intoxicating drinks.

He always put a screen between the outside and the inside sign of his business. He rejoiced at the thousands of delirium tremens patients that were carried to hospitals, or madly tore their way through the open door of Hell, reeking, foaming and screaming as they went down. The Saloon Devil loved crape, and rejoiced time after time as he saw it hanging from the doors of homes, wherein a son lay dead who had fallen down early under the Juggernaut wheels of Alcohol.

Whenever jails and penitentiaries were too small this same Demon laughed in ghoulish glee, and when fresh idiots were pushed into crowded asylums, he grinned with a satisfaction that was sickening and revolting to contemplate. Whenever a frenzied brain directed a murderer's hand to plunge a fatal knife or discharge a deadly weapon in the Saloon quarrel, this Saloon Devil would cry out as he saw the crimson heart's blood flowing in spurts: "That's my favorite color now, hurrah for blood red."

Such common spectacles as suffering and starving orphans and widows served to whet the appetite of this Demon as seasoning does in the food of mortals. If it ever happened that any one told him to stop his hellish business he would point with pride to his license neatly framed, and declare that he was doing an honorable business under the sanction of Uncle Sam. Just as honorable as the grocery or dry goods business.

No tongue or pen can portray the terribleness of this whole business. By reason of its withering effects, numberless efforts have been made by individuals to check the insolent advance of the Rum Devil. All these proved of but little account. The most effective work has been accomplished by one or another of the organizations having for their sole aim the overthrow of the Rum Devil.

One of the movements that has been, and is still endeavoring to destroy the Saloon Devil, is called Local Option. As this force marches towards the enemy, it finds that Uncle Sam and his soldiers are standing in defense of the whole liquor business. So Local Option, with much difficulty, must labor heavily to operate even on a small area at one time. Local Option would accomplish much more if it were not for the respectability with which uncle Sam has clothed the Saloon Devil.

One day the Saloon Devil noticed the army of W. C. T. U. and he told Uncle Sam that he dreaded that crowd of women about as much as anything else. "They are so sneaking in their work. Their indirect methods and roundabout ways, I fear, will do more to cut off my future supply of customers than anything else."

Uncle Sam looked down upon the Saloon Devil and asked him what he thought of the Prohibition Hosts that were advancing.

"I shudder with dread as I think of them, but so long as I can keep the church blinded to the value of a united move against me, I can smile at the few votes that fall like lead upon me. I have worked harder to keep the saloon question out of politics than you can imagine. I always urge people to pray and talk and wait. Every single vote that hits a saloon, hits me. Bless you, dear Uncle Sam, nothing makes me feel so safe before my enemies as your strong arm raised in protection over me."

"Yes, my son," said Uncle Sam, "and you shall have my strong arm so long as you pay me such large sums of money to carry on your business."

"What think you of the Anti-Saloon League that is arrayed against you?" further asked Uncle Sam.

"I could no more stand before them than I could before any of the other powers if it were not for your blessed hand, my dear Uncle. As long as you place your strong sanction of license authority upon my head, I shall feel safe from the armies that are moving upon me to bring about my destruction."

"As to the church I have but little fear inasmuch as the attack from that source is scattered. I must admit," smilingly continued the Devil, "that if the church forces were united that they could do eternal damage. I am even convinced that they would have the power to pull your hand off of my head."

"Never mind," said Uncle Sam, "just you go ahead creating widows and orphans, filling jails and almshouses, sending thousands to the penitentiary and killing thousands upon thousands every year. Just go ahead and blast the hearts and hopes of many. Continue your robbing, plundering and ruining. I will keep my hand upon your head until there are enough voters in my dominion who shall declare that you should no longer be clothed with respectable authority. Then, my son, I shall leave you to fight your battles alone and not until then."

How many people think that it would be a good thing to take away the hand of protection which covers the saloon and in its place let the verdict of condemnation fall upon it?

*If it were not for Uncle Sam, the Saloon Devil would be overthrown more easily.*
*Why does he protect it?*

## THE SALOON
### *The Devil's Doings*

IN the deepest recesses of the Under-World, where the blackest shadows congregate and the most fiendish plots are concocted,—there, in the heart of Sin's fortress, are the devices planned, the messages sent forth, that lure the young and unsuspecting into that most fatal of all traps— the licensed liquor saloon.

Other evils may have their seed-time and harvest, but the liquor traffic's crop is continually to be seen. From January till December— from the first day of spring till the last day of winter, this revolting crop of drunkards is being harvested ; the supply never runs short.

A million dollars would be a large sum to pour down the throats of a Christian nation, in any beverage that does harm and only harm; but what think you of twelve hundred and fifty millions thus wasted in our country every year!

This is an accurate estimate of the money expended annually for intoxicating liquors in America; to say nothing of the crimes and accidents resulting; the cost in dollars and cents and the uncounted cost in blood and tears.

Truly we should have far to look, to find a tyrant either in ancient or modern times that dared tax his subjects so heavily as King Alcohol taxes his meek and willing slaves, the American people!

Reader, which is worse, the historic tax on tea imposed by King George, which so aroused our forefathers' ire, or this tax that I have just named!

If I could have my way, there would be such a wholesale dumping of the products of brewery and still, into the waters of the Pacific or Atlantic, as would make the famous Boston tea party seem by contrast like a mere "tempest in a teapot." The freedom resulting from this new act of independence would be correspondingly greater. (Only, I should be sorry for the ocean!)

When will the American people learn to "stand up for their rights" enough to free themselves from this tremendous oppression? At present they submissively bow to the yoke of the liquor tyrant, and then complain when times are hard and wonder what the matter is. And the cost in dollars and cents is the least part of the damage done.

The saloons now multiplying in small towns and villages as well as large cities are a serious enough menace to the safety of our young people of a winter evening; but in summer the beer gardens are quite as dangerous, because if possible, even more enticing. One cannot pass along the street without continually thinking, "Another trap!"

How attractive are the beer gardens and dance halls fitted up! Yet the brilliant lights cast black shadows, darkening the entire lives of those who frequent such resorts.

In a temperance paper called "The Defender" has appeared a picture so striking that I shall have to describe it to you as best I may. It is called "A Midsummer Day's Reality."

In the centre is a church, of attractive modem build, but with doors and windows fast shut and a large placard across the front door, marked, "Closed until October 1st," while the minister is seen departing in hot haste carrying a valise marked "Europe."

In the foreground are grouped several representatives of the "powers that prey" on society, with bloated, leering faces, brandishing whiskey bottles and wine glasses and chorusing in high glee, "Bon voyage, sir pastor, bon voyage! We'll shepherd the flock." And encircling the church in the background are plainly visible a line of buildings into whose open doors the crowds are literally pouring. The first building is marked "Saloon. Open day and night." The next, "Dance Hall." The third, "Theatre," The fourth, "Continuous Vaudeville, 50 Female Beauties." The fifth bears a flag flying aloft on which is inscribed, "Roof Garden," while over the door is "Saloon." The sixth is a "Picture Parlor," with the price, "One Cent" conspicuously displayed; containing the penny slot machines and similar exhibits that will cram more filth into the mind in one minute than the church could remove in a year. And the last is a "Concert Hall" with "Beer" advertised on one window, and "Wines" on the other.

All open on a summer day, and doing a thriving business, while the church is resting!

Reader, what think you of this "Midsummer Day's Reality"! Is it overdrawn? Your own observation will tell you that it is not.

In the cities and larger towns this is a condition that confronts us— a serious, startling fact; and it affects the smaller towns in its results.

The educational and religious institutions are in midsummer largely out of business. The schools are closed; the Sunday schools have suspended; the church is shut up. The whole "plant" of those agencies that make for the elevation and refinement of society is closed down, for repairs possibly, but closed.

On the other hand, every agency that makes for degradation; the haunt of every vice; the gilded palace of every pleasure behind which hide the chains and slavery of the Shadow World, throw wide their doors—and many there be who go in thereat.

Think of the contrast; the closed churches along all the avenues of our cities, with placarded doors, silent bells, hushed organs and cobwebbed pulpits; the wide open "Fort Georges," "Coney Islands," "Beaches," "Points" and other resorts innumerable, where the brewer, the ginmiller and the purveyor to lust reap their harvests of bloody gold.

Don't flatter yourself with the idea that it is a local question for the cities alone to wrestle with. There is not a hamlet in the most secluded country-side to which the poison of hell's summer carnival will not filter.

Don't sit back complaisant and fancy that your home is so respectable and well guarded that this is not a matter of personal interest to you. A harvest of shame and disease and ruin will be reaped from the sowing of these summer months, not alone in the slums and in the homes of the unfortunate, but along the avenues and in thousands of homes where refinement and religion reign.

The picture of the closed church and open saloon faithfully reports the advance of a foe that menaces national life; of sappers who burrow beneath the very foundations of civilization. It is an inundation of ruin, a cataclysm of destruction, real, imminent, all-engulfing, that I would warn you of.

What can be done?

This at least: If the church must be closed, if the agencies of good must rest, there is neither necessity nor excuse for allowing the saloon and its foul consorts to assume sway. What place, at all, is there for such agencies in a state of society that calls itself civilization?

In my chapter on "Traps" I gave you a partial idea of the Bed Telephone fiend's methods of coaxing young men into saloons; yet the devices are so numerous that it would be impossible to name them all. The natural fondness of youth for gayety and social pleasures; the dread of being considered "odd" or "afraid" to drink; the lively music, the costly pictures, the elegant surroundings of the more pretentious saloons, and the games and cordial fellowship to be found even in the cheaper resorts; all these are used by the shadow-fiends with great effect. In later years the fiery, insatiable appetite is enough to draw these victims of drink to ruin. But before this craving is formed, the chief attraction is the love of a social time.

No young man would deliberately go into a saloon alone, for the first time, and drink; he is always drawn in by jovial companions. In this, then, lies the greatest danger to the individual. The strength of the social instinct is so great that the forces of evil make that side of human nature their special study; and so effectually have they done this that the churches, in their turn, must recognize the power of social recreation before the shadow-creatures can be completely outwitted.

Meanwhile let me say to every young man as he readies the point where his companions begin to urge these attractions of the saloon upon him: Do not heed them. Refuse all invitations to drink, at whatever cost. If to do this you have to part with friends, however reluctantly, the parting had better come; for the work of the saloon in a young man's life is too frightful to contemplate without a shudder.

A bright, ambitious young salesman, while "on the road," formed the habit of drinking with occasional customers and other "drummers," for the sake of sociability and to help his business, as he supposed. Returning to his home one night after drinking rather more freely than usual, he started a romp with his little brother, of whom he was very fond.

An unsteady lurching movement—an overturned lamp—and the result was, the room in flames, the house itself barely saved from destruction and his brother's face so burned that the scar was left for life. Had the young man been himself, the accident would never have occurred. It saddened his whole life.

Another young man, the son of a minister, allowed himself while away at college to he drawn into the habit of visiting saloons. He woke up from a drunken sleep one morning to find himself in jail, accused of killing one of his fellow-students in a street fight of which he had not the slightest recollection.

A third youth, brought up in a refined and cultured Christian home, fell in with several city youths who worked on his fondness for music to introduce him to social parties where wine was served. He soon learned to drink in saloons as well, and being of a nervous temperament, his downfall was rapid. He died of delirium tremens. And the horrors of such a death are too well known to require description.

Alcohol even in moderate quantities, it has been found, produces in a short time serious organic changes in the nerve cells of the brain and central nervous system. It also hinders the digestion of food, weakening the stomach and causing congestion, and very often leading to cancer.

Hence the argument that "alcohol is an aid to digestion" is the farthest possible from the truth. This and the other Red Telephone argument that "alcohol is a food" are too foolish to be taken seriously in this day of science. Some time ago, when the craze for Professor Atwater's theory was at its height, a drunken Swede was brought into a Chicago police court and made rather an amusing plea. He claimed that he 'had not been drinking, but eating, and as evidence, placed a small, half-filled bottle of "food" before the justice. He was asked what he meant by bringing whisky into the court.

"That is not whisky," said the prisoner. "That is food. I submit that you can not send me to the Bridewell for eating too much. Professor Atwater, of Wesleyan University, told the educational conference that whisky is food. He says you can not deny food value to whisky, and that it is oxidized just like bread and meat. When I read that, I got hungry and went out for a couple of slices of whisky and a piece of brandy."

"He had eaten a quart or two before I picked him up," said the policeman.

It is now known that the "food value" argument for alcohol has not the shadow of a foundation. Alcohol certainly has no useful place in the healthy body. It is a poison, and takes more lives annually in this country alone than almost all the acute infectious diseases put together.

The following is a partial list given by Hr. W. H. Riley of the many diseases caused by alcohol and which to a large degree at least might be prevented by abstaining from its use: Different forms of paralysis, epilepsy, apoplexy, general paralysis of the insane, delirium tremens, different forms of insanity, pneumonia, consumption of the lungs, different forms of indigestion, ulceration of the stomach, cancer of the stomach, Bright's disease of the kidneys, cirrhosis of the liver, fatty degeneration of the heart.

A formidable list; yet the Red Telephone voice will tell you that it will make you "feel better" to drink; that liquor is a tonic. Believe him at your peril. The feelings caused by alcohol are those of temporary exhilaration, followed by reaction, depression and disease. It is true now and always that "Wine is a mocker, strong drink is raging, and whosoever is deceived thereby is not wise."

Here is what Dr. Knoff, the consumption specialist, says of "Alcohol and the White Death":

"Alcoholism must be considered as the most active co-operator with the deadly tubercle bacillus, aside from being the greatest enemy to the welfare of a nation, the most frequent destroyer of family happiness, and the cause of the ruin of mind, body and soul. To combat alcoholism, education, above all, is required. From early childhood the dangers of intemperance and its fearful consequences should be taught, and alcohol should never be given to children, even in the smallest quantities."

The following, from the Soldier's Handbook, published by direction of the Secretary of War, is very significant:

"It should be unnecessary to speak of the danger from the use of intoxicating liquors, for every soldier knows something of this. The mind of a man under the influence of these liquors is so befogged that he is unable to protect himself from accidents and exposures. How many men have passed from this world because of exposures during intoxication? How many have lost their health and strength and become wretched sufferers during the remainder of a shortened existence? Besides, for days after indulgence in liquor the system is broken down and the individual less able to stand the fatigue, exposures, or wounds of the campaign."

The result of the war between Japan and Russia called forth many comments, but its most important lesson is in regard to temperance. Says Collier's Weekly:

"The Japanese were worried for months by the fewness of their battleships, but in the end they won, not by numbers but by morality —by sobriety, devotion, courage, and intelligence. They did not win by talk and bluster either. They have shown, in peace and war, a calm fair-mindedness, a predominating taste, a hostility to mere noise and thunder, an ability to be quiet, and mind their business, whether that business be art, domestic labor, or deadly war."

The Toronto Globe also found an interesting significance in the outcome of the war. "The result is in reality," it says, "the triumph of sober Japan over whisky-soaked Russia. It is the greatest temperance lecture ever delivered to the world, to nations and to individuals as well.

"What was proved on the wreck-strewn Straits of Corea had already been proved in the destruction of the Port Arthur squadron, in the running fight with the Vladivostock cruisers, in the reduction of an almost impregnable fortress, and in the land operations in Manchuria. It was in each case Japan against Russia, but it was more It was temperance against debauchery "Japan's achievements on land and sea were not directed by men who had spent their days and nights in idleness and dissipation. They were the product of lives of strong, steadfast, sober endeavor, the very opposite of what their enemy had been.

"The lesson of the war is not for Russia alone. It is for every nation and for every individual who seeks stability and advancement. Intemperance and progress do not go together."

*"Wine is a mocker; strong drink is raging and whosoever is deceived thereby is not wise."*

## THE DEVIL'S LABORATORY
### *The Devil of Today*

As I prayed, my vision cleared and I saw Satan in the laboratory of his castle home.

He was in an apartment on the upper floor. Light streamed through many windows upon lines of retorts from which were steadily dropping into huge receptacles green liquors of varying shades. Bottles labeled Envy or Jealousy were piled conveniently near, and, at a word from the Archfiend, a small army of assistants filled them from the vessels he indicated.

### SATAN MIXES HIS OWN POISONS

I marvelled somewhat that Satan allowed no one but himself to mix the poisons that fed the retorts, but now, as at other times in my dream, there came to me what I would know. It was as though one standing by my side had whispered:

"Since time was, he has suffered no hands but his own to mix his death-dealing potions."

As my eyes swept around the room, they now rested upon those who were making up the poisons for shipment. Each package contained one bottle of Envy and one of Jealousy, and bore the name of the person who was to receive it, and the destination as well.

Then I heard Satan say, as he picked up a bottle labelled Envy, "A little of this will poison any heart, and no one knows what ends it may achieve. But," he continued, taking up another bottle, with Jealousy upon the label, "used together, these can neutralize more Christian virtues than any decoctions I have ever brewed. Cain was the first to take them, and from his time to the present day, they have never failed me."

### THE THOUGHTS OF CHRISTIANS MUST BE POISONED

Turning to a group of fiends who stood apart from the workmen, Satan said:

"It is time to be about your work! In some way you must get these drops into the hearts of Christians, and it behooves you to administer them with the utmost care, else they will be refused.

"Never mention my name in connection with your work," he went on. "Watch for opportunities, and when people are admiring the blessings and possessions of others, inject these poisons into their hearts.

"This will create a longing for the things they see, and that longing will grow into a wish, and with the wish a spirit of envy, and envy, when it hath conceived, shall give birth to jealousy," he explained.

"Your orders shall be obeyed," the leader of the band answered, and silently they went out upon their unholy mission.

As I wondered if there were any to give warning to the children of men, I was taken, still in my vision, to the home of Widow Faith.

"And the Angel of his presence saved them," said Widow Faith as she sat in her modest home. Sacrifice on every hand attended her path, and her deprivations in life were accentuated in view of the fact that her younger days had been spent in affluence and comfort.

## SATAN'S EMISSARY VISITS THE WIDOW'S HOME

She had that day especially noted the plentitude of the rich, and was longing that her children might have more of the luxuries of Life. A spirit which approached resentment, arose unbidden in her heart, and she sought to smother it.

"I must not suffer these thoughts to thus engage my mind," she said to herself. "Envy and covetousness are not the marks of a Christian."

She sat for a moment in silence, as the tears coursed down her face, and fell upon her little child asleep in her arms.

"Father in Heaven give me a clean and murmurless spirit," she pleaded, "for Thou hast filled my life with good things."

## THE FIEND WHISPERS A LIE

Then it was that one of the fiends whispered to her: "This is a false way by which to view life. Why should you suffer deprivations while others, less worthy, are having triple their share of good things?"

She listened to the logic of the suggestion for a moment, not knowing from whence it came.

"Why should I and my children be deprived of what I need? Have I deserved it? I've tried hard all these years to walk in God's way," said she to herself. "Oh, that I had—"

The fiend was preparing to inject the poison and would have succeeded had it not been for divine intervention.

## THE ANGEL BRINGS CONTENTMENT

"Let your conversation be without covetousness; and be content with such things as ye have," whispered the Good Angel, "for hath He not said, 'I will not leave thee, nor forsake thee?'"

Widow Faith hesitated for a moment, and then arose. As she went to her task, it was with the content that the Angel had given, and she found herself saying: "Be not overcome of evil, but overcome evil with good."

The Angel tarried in the house until the fiend with his hurtful poison had withdrawn, and as he left the home he had endeavored to harm, she heard him mutter:

"I failed because of that Angel's whisper."

"I would have sinned," said Widow Faith to herself, "had God not strengthened me by His words," and, looking up she breathed a prayer of thanksgiving, little knowing the contest that had been waged about her trusting soul.

As the Angel turned to leave this home, I heard her say:

"Dear Father, suffer not the Evil One to corrupt this heart with a spirit of envy. Keep her from the poison of this sin!"

And the Lord answered, "I will keep her as the apple of mine eye."

## THE POISON FIENDS TELL THEIR STORY

The Angel in thousands of instances had counteracted the poison of Envy and Jealousy; and the Devil's scheme to taint the souls of men with baneful poisons was now well known abroad.

In consequence a great number were rendered proof against his subtlety.

As the fiends to whom the poison had been entrusted were returning to the castle, I saw that they were much dejected in spirit and reluctant to appear before their master, because of their ill success. Soon they entered the dense shrubbery for conference, and as a result agreed to cover their failure, as far as possible, with a lie.

"We have given these poisons a fair trial," said one.

"We certainly have," added another.

"It is no fault of ours if people refuse to take them," said a third.

"His Majesty must be reasonable in this matter," said a fourth.

Then they set out for the castle with hesitating steps, and Satan met them at the gate.

"What have you to report?" he gruffly asked.

"Rather poor success," answered the foremost one.

"What?" ejaculated Satan angrily.

"It is not our fault," ventured another. "We gave the poisons a fair test, but the people refused to take them."

"By whose advice?" inquired Satan.

"The Angel, and one known as Evangelist, opposed them vigorously," was the reply.

## THE DRUNKARD
*The Sight of Hell*

Do you hear that man roaring out in the middle of Hell? How loud his voice is. It rises above all the groans, and shrieks, and cries, and screams, of millions. With a voice like thunder he roars out: "Oh, a drop of cold water, a drop of cold water to cool my tongue; my tongue is thirsty, my tongue is burning, my tongue is red-hot. Give me a drop of cold water, only one single drop of cold water to cool my burning tongue." The devil answers his roar with another roar: "You fool," he says, "you drunkard, why do you cry out for cold water to cool your burning tongue; there is no cold water in Hell." Still the drunkard goes on roaring for a drop of cold water. Now the devil lifts up a scourge of fire to strike him and make him hold his tongue. Then the drunkard sinks down into a deep pool of fire and brimstone, where he is drowned in destruction and perdition.

You drunkards, who on Saturday evenings are in the public-house, and on Sundays away from Mass; you drunkards, whose children are hungered and in rags, and go neither to Catechism nor Mass, go down to Hell, and listen to your brother-drunkard crying out for a drop of cold water to cool his burning tongue!

## GAMBLING AMONG "FASHIONABLE SOCIETY."
### *Palaces of Sin*

To the uninitiated country man and woman, who have been brought up to look upon the sin of gambling as one of the most degrading things imaginable, they will hardly believe that members of "Fashionable Society'^ with scarcely an exception, are inveterate gamblers, but nevertheless such is the case.

What I will relate in this chapter is not what I have heard, but is what I have seen with my own eyes, and I frankly acknowledge that I had associated with this class of people for so long, that I was made to become one of this unholy class.

You will often hear "Society folks" talk about

"Euchre parties," but you will never hear them acknowledge they gamble, and it is a known fact among those who have associated with this class of people, that they not only gamble for small amounts, but they will wager large amounts, and the only difference between the ^'Fashionable Gambling" houses and what you would call a "Gambling Den" is, that these "Gambling Dens" are subject to raid by the officers of the law, for they make no pretense of being anything but gambling houses.

However, upon the other hand, "Fashionable Society" does not have as much respect for their individual homes as the vilest kind of a gambler, for this "Fashionable" herd will open up a game of chance right in their own parlors, which renders them almost immune from arrest, by the police officer that travels their beat, for two reasons. First, the policeman does not know that gambling is being carried on in this elegant mansion in the fashionable part of a city, and the second reason why their houses are not raided the same as that of common gamblers is, because should such a move be put on foot, they will hush it up with their millions.

I remember distinctly the first time I ever saw a game of what is called "Draw Poker" played in my life, as in my boyhood days my dear old father and mother taught me to believe that card playing was not right, and that gambling was the most degrading thing that a young man could get in the habit of doing, therefore, when my fortune was left me by my old aunt, I was ignorant of any game of cards, in fact I did not know one card from the other.

Soon after reaching the City of Washington, I was invited by one of my gentleman (?) friends, to call at his house, as he stated they were going to have a little game of cards for amusement.

I told him I knew nothing about cards, for I had never played a game of cards in my life, and he seemed to be very much astonished at my "ignorance." You may call it "ignorance" if you like, but T would consider it a great compliment to have the world know that I had never seen a game of cards played. However such can not be the case, as my first lessons in such matters were unheeded, but thank God my "second sight," as it were, has returned to me and the teachings of my youth looms up before me with wonderful power.

I called upon this young gentleman (?) after supper, and about ten o'clock an ivory topped table was wheeled to the center of the room and the other guests were invited to "set around." There were others there besides myself, not only gentlemen but ladies, and when the ladies deliberately took their places around this ivory topped "Implement of Hell" called by "Society" a "Poker Table" I was indeed astonished, as I had only gotten an introduction to these ladies that evening, therefore I was surprised to know how familiar they could become on such short notice, but my greatest wonderment seized me when my young gentleman friend wanted to know what the ^"limit" would be. I knew nothing about what "Poker" was, neither did I know what "limit" meant, only I imagined there must be an element of chance attached to its meaning, but I at that time considered it would be a disgrace to let this elegant (?) "Society" know that I was a "Tenderfoot" in the ways of the Devil, so I pushed up my chair like an "old timer," of course not thinking for a moment that I was to be robbed by my friends in their own homes.

I resolved that there was no better time in the world for me to learn how to play "Poker" than at that time, so I kept a keen lookout for a few moments until I got the run of the game, at the same time I was bewildered by the expressions of "ante," "limit," "Jackpot" and such other language as is used among the gambling fraternity, but within half an hour I had been made familiar with what these names meant. My female associates manipulated the cards and used the language of the game with much ease.

I, of course, had but very little money with me, perhaps a couple of hundred dollars, but I never dreamed that I had been invited to this elegant mansion, which was the home of "Fashionable Society" to participate in a game where the predominating spirit was MONEY, as I believed when I received the invitation that it was to be a social game of cards for pastime, never dreaming there was to be a money consideration.

After the game had started and I learned they were playing for money, the thought struck me that it would be for only a small amount, and just enough to "make the game interesting" as the "Society lady" calls it, but before we had gone far, I realized the fact that these elegant gentlemen (?) and those perfumed ladies (?) were out for no other purpose than to make money.

At first I won a little money, but after a while I began to have to visit my pocket-book very frequently, and before eleven o'clock it was empty, and I was short something like One Hundred and Seventy-five or Two Hundred Dollars. I had my check book in my pocket, and I asked them if any one would cash my check for Five Hundred Dollars, which accommodation I soon received.

Within a short time my elegant "Society" friends played for big stakes and before I left that gambling den, about four o'clock in the morning, I had not only spent the One Hundred and Seventy-five or Two Hundred Dollars in cash that I brought with me, but I had issued my checks for over Seven Thousand Dollars.

Where had it gone, and who had received this money?

Oh, no one but my elegant friends (?) who had invited me to their home and robbed me with as little compunction of conscience as the highwayman with masked face would take your money from you at the point of his revolver.

I had learned to play "Poker" and paid well for my first lesson.

Had I have had as much sense as a "load of old shoes" I, right then and there, would have turned my back on "Fashionable Society," but the glitter of gold and the flash of their diamonds had so bewildered me that I was almost as helpless to leave these "Palaces of Sin" as the poor moth is, to pull herself away from the bright blaze of the candle.

To my certain knowledge Miss Etta Bartley, who was the Niece of a Senator, received over Two Thousand Dollars of my poor old Aunt's money, and if any one would have called Miss Etta Bartley a gambler, she would have died with heart disease in four minutes.

I never knew for a certainty, but I will always believe that that game of "Poker" was a set up job on me, and that I was deliberately robbed of my money, however, I could not prove this to be true, but I know one thing, and that is this, that I got exactly what was due me, and I have no sympathy for any man who has not manhood and sense enough to refuse to drink poison, when he knows that it is poison.

I have had several invitations to play "Poker" since that night, and have accepted one or two invitations, but never lost any great amount of money, as I soon learned that these "Society" people played "Poker" for what there was in it, in fact, they make it a business and at least one-fourth of these butterflies of fashion, who parade as "pure women," obtain their finery by the degrading practice of gambling.

You may not know it, but the majority of our Congressmen and Senators whom we send to Washington City play "Poker," and other games of chance, and they do not play them for pastime, but they actually play for money, but they would tell you they only played for "fun."

No man or woman that lives can indulge in an evil "for fun" and make a practice of this evil and not leave the taint of sin upon them, as it would be just as impossible to empty a cup of filthy water into a bucket of pure spring water, and leave it as clear afterwards as before, as it would be to follow the ways of the sinner and not become sinful.

We find gambling among our (church members, as they will give these "Euchre Parties," which are the Devil's own institution, and will charge each one who participates in the game a fee of 25 or 50 cents and will give a prize to the one who wins the most games.

This money they collect as a "fee" for playing the games, goes to the Church. Think of it, money obtained in this manner being donated and used by a Church which holds Christ and Him crucified up to the sinner as an example, when the members will resort to such ungodly methods to obtain money; and the preacher, be it said to his everlasting disgrace, often smiles upon such actions.

The trouble with the American people and in fact all other nations is, that they endeavor to "mimic" the actions of the wealthy, and you will find the "common people" giving "Euchre Parties" for the benefit of the Church, simply because they want to impress their neighbors that they are "up-to-date" and doing what "Fashionable Society" does, and just as long as the "common people" try to follow the footsteps of "Fashionable Society" just that long humanity will be degraded, for any man or woman who will try to keep pace with this "renegade tribe of the Devil's own" just that long sin, vice, and immorality will remain to curse us.

Be it said to the everlasting credit of those who live in the country and in smaller towns, they do not practice the abominations found in larger cities, and the man or woman who would endeavor to introduce these scandalous practices in the country would be treated as a person to be dreaded, and abhorred and dangerous to the morals of any neighborhood. Such would be a righteous judgment, for you can not set the proper example before the young and follow exactly the same practices and customs as the young knows the sinner to follow.

"Fashionable Society" always plays the part of morality, decency and Christianity, as they have long since learned that in order to more easily lead the "common people" in their trail of debauchery, they must play the part of "saint."

If it is wrong for the keeper of a "bar-room" to have gambling in his establishment, it is wrong for "society" to gamble in her mansions. If it is wrong for the poor man to drink wine from the counter of the "common saloon" it is an abomination for the wealthy to drink it from their ivory topped tables. If it is a sin for the laboring man to obtain the money of his associates by the degrading practice of gambling, it is a sin for the diamond bedecked hand of wealth to take the money in the same manner from her associates.

There is no sin that will contaminate and sink into perdition the soul of the poor man, that will not eternally damn the soul of the rich.

I have visited homes where extravagant elegance was visible upon every hand, and where they presumed to set the example of fashion, of morals and of politeness to the '^common people,'^ when if the laboring man, the mechanic or the merchant would endeavor to follow their example, he would not only wreck his business and wreck his character, but would eternally damn his soul and would be looked upon as a character that no decent man or woman could afford to pattern after.

I remember being in Philadelphia, visiting some of this "highly perfumed set" and received an invitation to a "card party" to be given at the home of one of "Society's followers" and of course like a "truckling fool" that I was, I went. However, by this time I had learned that "Card Parties" and "Euchre Parties" and anything that had "cards" attached to it, meant nine times out of ten that gambling would be the order of the day, but I am glad to say that I had been taught a lesson in cards that I had not forgotten; in fact gambling was one of society's sins that did not interest me a particle and the only reason that I was persuaded into it was on the account of trying to "look smart" and not having moral courage to say "NO."

My friends and I called that evening at the home of our friends where the "card party" was to be given, and of course "elegant society" (?) was there in all of her grandeur, and the Devil also was there with his paraphernalia of Hell, his wine, champagne, cards and every other sin known to the vocabulary of the Devil.

After an hour of silly prattle by all of us, the presiding lady of that home gently pulled down the blinds of that splendid double parlor, which meant as I had long since learned, that a card game was about to open in "full blast." I think there was something like six or seven ladies and about as many gentlemen who sat around that Ivory Topped Table to play "Poker" like inveterate gamblers.

This class of people invariably commence by playing for a penny or not more, than live cents, which is done in order to entice every one of the party to "take a hand" and this innocent looking pastime generally entices all of the party to "set up" to the table.

"Society" well knows if she can get one of her "dupes" started in the game that they would feel humiliated to drop out, which will enable the most scientific of the game to fleece the unsuspecting "Fashionable idiot."

"This card party" was near the farthest end of my society career and I was not very particular whether they liked me or not, as I had about come to the conclusion that the whole thing was an abomination and a disgrace to mankind, therefore I had become more outspoken in regard to my likes and dislikes and I could say with considerable emphasis, consequently when one of these sweet faced Devils of "Society" with her bewitching smile says "Col. Maple, aren't you going to play with us?" I bluntly said "No, as I had had my eye-teeth cut long since," which seemed to considerably disturb the "painted countenance" of my "she beauty." However, I was not particular whether she liked it or not, and I took no part in the game, but sat by as an interested spectator and gazed upon the cunning and disreputable practices of this "Society gang" in order to obtain money from their associates.

It has always seemed to me that the women of "Society" were better players than the men, or at least, they always won more money than the male contingent, and I was unable to discern whether it was actually because they were better players or better thieves, and before that game was over I was pretty well convinced that it was on the account of the ladies (?) being better thieves than the gentlemen, for I sat around that "Ivory topped Table" and beheld schemes and tricks that would have cost a professional gambler his life, had his villainy been detected by his associates.

One of the ladies who was engaged in this game was a Miss Orton from the State of Ohio, and who I understood was quite wealthy.

This girl lost heavily that night and from her deep concern in the game, and from the look of despair when she would lose, would lead any one to believe that her finances were at least getting towards the point where the loss of money hurt, as she became nervous and "rattled" and drank wine and champagne with the recklessness of a toper, but you must bear in mind, kind reader, that wine and champagne is a bosom companion in all of these gambling socials among the rich, for wine is used for a stimulant and as the motive power which forces the "Moneyed fool" to lose his cash for the benefit of the "wise ones," therefore it would be impossible to systematically rob their companions without the use of alcoholic stimulants.

Miss Orton had lost quite a little fortune, perhaps Fifteen Hundred or Two Thousand Dollars, when she burst into tears and stated that she did not have another cent with her, and would not draw her check for another dollar, as she was in "bad luck," but bantered any man around the table to play her "One Hundred Dollars against a kiss." Of course these "biped imps" were forced to be gallant and the challenge was accepted, and a young man by the name of Earley accepted the proposition, and this poor girl lost again, and brazenly before her companions paid the debt.

In my estimation she might as well have gambled her virtue against the $100.00 as to have done what she did, for it was a step in that direction, to say the least of it.

If the devotees of "Fashionable Society" who claim the right of setting the example for the masses, are so corrupt as to resort to every deception known to the lowest class of mankind, then pray tell me the difference between the two, with the exception, however, of one class having money and the other not.

A man or woman who will sit around the table with this tribe of fashion, and who plays in their games can not detect their tricks and schemes they resort to in order to win your money, but if you will sit by as a spectator you can readily understand why some are more "lucky" than others, as in fact there is no such a thing as "luck" to the gambling fraternity or "Fashionable Society," as they will not trust "fickle luck" for their success, but they resort to tricks which are considered disreputable by wide open "Gambling Dens" and any man who would practice such trickery in one of them and it was found out upon him, he would either pay the penalty with his life, or be the recipient of a huge thrashing.

This "Fashionable tribe" had to learn these tricks from some one, as they do not present themselves to any one in a beautiful nightly vision. Now if they had to be taught these tricks called the "Gambler's art" they had to gain their information from some "Red handed" frequenter of "Gambling Dens" and if "Society" will stoop so low as to practice upon her associates the schemes and tricks that she learned from the lowest characters on earth, then what right has this "brazen jade" to claim the right to set the example for humanity?

Whenever I hear of a "Euchre Party" or "Card party," I wonder what the mothers and fathers of this land can mean by permitting their pure girls and their noble sons to attend them, for it is in the Parlors of "Fashionable Society" and the ones who try to "mimic" her, that the first principles for the mania of gambling is founded, and where the first lessons of Harlotism, vice and degradation is instilled in the minds of the young.

The sins of the drunkard in the gutter have no attraction for the young, as they consider them an abomination. The blear eyed countenance of the disreputable woman and her profane language have no attraction for the young. No sin that is committed by the lowest element of the universe attracts the attention and admiration of the young man and woman, but Ah! where the trouble lies is the sins committed by what the world calls the "Leaders of Society" with her gaudy apparel and rich equippage, for the young man and woman of this country try to imitate this class, they believing that it is the "proper thing" simply because wealth is permitted to go unrebuked.

I could mention, I suppose, fifty different experiences that I have had with this 'fashionable Gang" where the magnificent parlors of their mansions were turned into "Gambling Hells."

I would advise the fathers and mothers of this land to look with as much contempt upon the "Euchre Parties" and "Card Parties" given by their neighbors and by the Church members, as they would upon the open "Gambling Dens" attached to the bar rooms, for these "Euchre Parties" and "Card Socials" are the stepping stones that leads to the misery incidental to the crime of Gambling. When sin and immorality committed by the rich and "Fashionable Society" is punished in the same manner, as when committed by the poor wretch of God's universe, then the young and rising generation will learn that sin and immorality is an abomination and the destroyer of character regardless of whether it is committed by the pauper in rags, or the millionaire in his "purple and fine linen."

## WHY THE JOKE FAILED
### *The Devil's Doings*

FEW things are better medicine than a good laugh. Even the Northeast Man would find life taking on a rosy tinge if he would make it a rule to find something to laugh about, half-a-dozen times a day ; for the right kind of laugh will do far more to drive the shadow-creatures away than the wrong kind of sermon.

Yes, a good laugh is well worth while. Many of the best and greatest men in the world 's history have possessed a strong sense of humor; and the preachers who can stir men's hearts most deeply are always those whose faces show the pleasant, mirthful lines belonging only to those who have a keen appreciation of a good joke. The sense of humor is a gift not to be despised, and if any person is so unfortunate as to be deficient in this gift, let him not think it a waste of time to cultivate it.

> "Smile, once in a while!
> 'Twill make your heart seem lighter.

Smile once in a while;
'Twill make your pathway brighter.
Life's a mirror; if we smile,
Smiles come back to greet us;
If we're frowning all the while,
Frowns forever meet us."

This is true philosophy, and religion, too. Yes, there is ten times as much genuine religion in a hearty laugh as there is in a frown.

The important thing to make sure of, in this connection, is that the laugh is free from the faintest suggestion of malice or ill-nature.

If there is any ill-nature in a laugh—any desire to make another person needlessly uncomfortable—it might as well be a frown. It is not a genuine laugh at all; only a weak or coarse imitation. And the sort of pleasure it brings the one who indulges in it is not the genuine thing, either. It tries sometimes to make up in noise what it lacks in real mirthfulness. Did you ever notice the rasping, choking, harsh quality of the mirthless laugh of sarcasm or malice? It is a sound which only the shadow-creatures can teach in its full hideousness.

Directly opposed to this is the laugh of pure, innocent delight, such as the merriment of a little child. Is there any sweeter music on earth than a child's ringing laughter? It is like the song of the wood-birds and the rippling of a brook, blended in one. It is blessedly contagious; and a great deal of this irresistible, mirth-provoking magic can be retained even as the voice loses its childish tones. It depends on the kind of soul—the kind of Self—that is doing the laughing.

A sense of humor is one of the greatest helps over the hard places in life. Countless times have I given thanks from the depths of my heart that I had been blessed with the power of seeing the humorous side of a trying situation. It turns clouds into sunshine on many occasions when a more serious view would have meant only, at best, a dull resignation to unavoidable discomfort, or an enforced patience with ignorance or rudeness almost beyond human endurance. Treat an attempted insult as a joke and you rob it of all its force, and in so doing, "turn the laugh" most effectually, but harmlessly, on the one guilty of the intended discourtesy. If he is wise, he will accept the same humorous view of the matter and be thankful to get off so easily, while it will put his own ill-humor to shame and often disperse it altogether, far more readily than could any serious argument. If one has wit enough to meet ill-natured tricks in this way, it is ten to one that in thus substituting a good joke for a poor one the way is cleared for a better understanding and a better feeling all around. Blessed is humor! especially when the joke is on the humorist!

Two boys at boarding-school resolved to play an "April fool" joke on the authorities. The plan was as follows: Both these brilliant youths were to feign sickness, get excused toward evening and go early to their rooms. Meanwhile they were to confide (apparently) in the little twelve-year-old sister of one of the instructors, giving her to understand that they meant to slip away at nine o'clock that evening for a revel in a down-town bake-shop. She would give the alarm, of course, and there was a delightful picture in the minds of the two young scamps of the fruitless search to be made by the irate teachers for the supposed run-aways who would be all the time safe in their beds.

The preparations were most successful in every detail so far as known to the plotters. They were both seized with the most heart-rending coughs, found time between lessons and coughing to drop their hint as planned, and dragged their way wearily around until eight o'clock, when permission to retire was readily granted them. But the sequel was a decided disappointment to the astonished would-be jokers. Little sister had not played the tell-tale in exactly the way expected, and the result was that instead of frantic professors searching the streets in vain, there was a visit from an extremely business-like doctor, two of the most thoroughly-dosed patients ever seen, and a serene, sympathetic, motherly nurse, self appointed, to sit up with the unfortunates until midnight and see that they did not miss taking their medicine! The affairs of the school went on as usual, while the two April jokers were soothingly assured by the housekeeper that their illness would soon be relieved, thanks to the "thoughtfulness of that dear child, who was so worried by their coughs that she insisted on going for the doctor herself!" Whether the harmless but awful-tasting stuff prescribed fully cured them of their fondness for practical jokes or not, need hardly be recorded. We can safely guess that it was some time before they would relish another attempt of precisely the same kind.

Another case comes to my recollection, in which the jokers fared quite as unfortunately. Two young men took it into their heads that they would prepare a surprise for some friends of theirs, a newly married couple who were about to start housekeeping in a cozy city flat.

The two jokers, whom we will call Smith and Jones because those were not their names, thought it would be fine fun to go into the flat and re-arrange the furniture according to their own peculiar tastes. They did so. It was necessary to break a lock, but that, they flattered themselves, could be easily repaired after the fun was over. They found everything in apple-pie order. When they had been there an hour, it was—well, otherwise. The tinware was piled up in a pyramid on the lace cover of the best bed; the pictures hung with their faces to the walls; the dishes were arrayed in rows on the piano; the dining-table was loaded with books, bric-a-brac and a small rug or two; a hassock reposed on the mantel, and a mirror on the floor. Altogether they made a com-plete job of their rearrangements, and when it was time for the bride and groom to arrive, Smith and Jones proceeded to carry out the last number on their elaborate program by hiding in a clothes-closet from which, after enjoying the first astonished exclamations of their friends, they intended to burst out upon them as a climax to the surprise.

Alas! the surprise took an entirely unexpected turn. The voices whose startled and wrathful tones reached the ears of the concealed jokers were not the voices of their friends, but of perfect strangers. There had been a miscalculation somewhere—and sad to relate, it was not a mistake of the people who had returned to their apartment. They were in the right flat—but Smith and Jones were not!

With slowly rising hair and chattering teeth the would-be jokers took in the full horrors of the situation. They had mistaken the num-ber of the flat, had broken into one belonging to strangers, and in-stead of a merry time setting things to rights again they were in danger of having the opportunity to explain their unheard-of conduct at the nearest police court. How, indeed, could they hope to be believed?

There was no escape from discovery. Soon the angry tenant of the apartment flung open the closet door and at the point of a revolver the two supposed burglars were invited to come out. They accepted the invitation. It took all their powers of eloquence to persuade their in-censed host not to telephone immediately for the police, but finally the matter was explained, if not satisfactorily, at least sufficiently so that the disgusted tenant allowed them to go, after forcing them, still at the point of a revolver, to put everything back exactly where they found it, and pay for the broken lock. Meanwhile the bride and groom were contentedly enjoying their own undisturbed! flat a block away, never dreaming of the commotion caused by their not having been burglarized by their (joke)-loving friends. Smith and Jones tried hard to keep the secret, but of course, it leaked out; such things always do; and the bride and groom, with all their friends, were not slow in appreciating the humor of the situation. The joke was certainly a success!

Somehow, there is no joke relished half so keenly as the joke turned against the jokers. It is in part, perhaps, humanity's love of fair play which causes this enjoyment; yet it may be something more. We shall see, presently. But, although we may regard the joke as a success in both the above instances, we must remember that the would-be jokers did not. From their point of view the joke was a most humiliating failure. Now, why did it fail?

Because in both cases it was based on a wrong idea of enjoyment —a perverted sense of humor. It was based on the idea that a false alarm, causing panic and consternation, can be a source of innocent pleasure.

Nothing can give true pleasure that is based on giving trouble to others. The enjoyment that results or seems to result from such a course, would not always, it is true, be turned so quickly and noticeably into a crestfallen embarrassment as in the two cases I have named. But even where an ill-natured joke appears to succeed, it has a result not seen on the surface—the result of harm to the reputation and real character of the joker.

Slight or great, according to the nature of the thing done, is the mischief wrought. In fact, however, we cannot always tell in advance what will prove of slight and what of transcendent importance. More than once has a fine opportunity in life been lost because the young person to whom it was about to be offered was found to be too fond of coarse, silly jokes to be entrusted with business requiring tact, a delicate sense of propriety and a fine consideration for the feelings of others. In such a case, truly, the joking leads to failure rather than to success.

Again, there is no joke that is so certain a failure as that indulged in with the intent to deceive or frighten children. I only wish my pen could express one-half the disgust, the utter loathing that every rightly-constituted human being has towards the unfeeling, cowardly idiot who will take a fancied pleasure in frightening a little child. No words can do justice to this subject. But let me at least warn all who ever have an impulse to torture and distress the little ones, that they are taking a terrible risk. Many a child has been frightened into convulsions, brain fever or lifelong insanity by the horrible stories or grotesque pranks supposed by their contrivers at the time to be "a good joke." The long list of tragedies resulting from the playful pointing of a pistol, with the invariable excuse given afterwards, "I didn't know it was loaded," is no worse than the fact of homes darkened by the cruel thoughtlessness of someone who imagined it would be fine fun to make sport of the innocent trustfulness of a little child.

Yes, a joke based on a sudden shock or fright to the weak, is always a failure and often leads to the keenest remorse for the harm done which can never be undone.

Another form of joke which can be relied on to fail every time, is the habit of jesting with things sacred. Religion, love, womanhood, marriage, the constancy of friends, the shyness of young people just learning the meaning of life's deepest mysteries, the loving devotion of a mother, the very beginnings of so wonderful and divine a thing as life itself—how did these topics ever become the subject for the rude jests of the unthinking? That shows that there is yet in the world a vast deal of ignorance, which can only lead to shame and suffering. To jest coarsely and laugh loudly over some proof of deep human emotion, whether it be of grief, worship or tenderness, is like tearing to pieces a delicate flower of priceless value. Nothing so surely stamps a person as out of harmony with the pure joys of a right life, as to try to find pleasure from ridiculing sacred things. It is a failure, and a disgraceful one.

It will be found, then, that the jokes which fail are of three kinds: those which are ill-natured, those which aim at frightening the weak, and those which would cast ridicule on things sacred. All these result from listening to the Red Telephone imp who tries to pervert the God-given sense of pure, delicious humor into a grim mockery; which brings pain rather than pleasure, loss rather than gain, and remorseful memories of wasted hours which might have been spent in building up joys instead of sorrows.

For, be it remembered, the sense of humor as God gave it, is divine. It brings health, sunshine, joy into the life wherever it is admitted. A good joke is one that surprises and delights without hurting; that leaves a good taste in the mouth and a sense of pure refreshment in the soul. The words "Just for fun" so often heard over the wires of the

Red Telephone, could be made a message of cheer instead of terror, to thousands of weary lives, and by so doing, the joker would experience a thrill of delight utterly unknown to him before.

In a charming Christmas play for children, written by Mattie-Marie Gamble, appears an odd, clever, little goblin from Dreamland whose name is Fun. "I took that name," he explains, "because, you see, people are always doing things 'just for fun' and so I thought I would be well taken care of!" And truly, if all fun-impulses were as pure and helpful as his, the world would be the better for taking care of them, and encouraging them wherever found. Would that some such kind and merry goblin could be always at hand in trying times, to enlighten and amuse! And in fact, we need not idly wish for such help. We have it already, within our own hearts, waiting for cultivation and encouragement.

I believe, and I repeat it here with all reverence, that the Divine sense of humor is unlimited; that man has never yet sounded the depths of this part of God's nature. Truly the angels must have many opportunities, with their larger and keener vision than man's, to see the quaint, delicious, humorous side of the vast panorama of life spread out before them. Where we see only the sad side of things, their eyes must be stronger and can look through the troubles to the joy beyond, the beautiful pattern that is being worked out. How amused they must be sometimes at the way man in his childishness frets and fumes, scolds and struggles at the very agencies which are bringing him blessing! And to God, who can see so much that even the angels cannot,—does it never seem that even He must smile at the twisted notions, the curious little blunders, of human beings who fancy that they "know it all" and can foretell His movements, if not, indeed, improve on His work? Does He not often, in fact, display this gentle, infinitely tender, yet infinitely great sense of humor in His very ways, as unexpected as they are effectual, of answering human prayer?

Surely this glimpse of an attribute so seldom recognized in the Divine nature cannot fail to make us love our Father more and serve Him better than ever before, for it makes our kinship to Him the more vitally real to our minds. In the conversation of Jesus, in his quick-witted answers to questions intended to entrap him, and in his parables, every observer will find ample proof that a keen humorous understanding of man's childish follies and inconsistencies is not out of keeping with a love so great that it would die for the object of its expression. Let us, then, revere and cultivate this divine sense of humor, and make of it our chief protection against the alluring suggestions of the shadow-jokers at the Red Telephone. Their attempts at wit and humor lead to sure humiliation and remorse. Christ's way leads to life and health of the whole nature. To choose the kind of humor that brings the most lasting pleasure is surely the part of wisdom.

*The road to crime.*

## THE ROAD TO CRIME
### *The Devil's Doings*

EVEN Boston's bewildering network of streets cannot compare in crookedness and intricacy with the lanes, highways and byways of the Under-World. There, among the haunts of the shadow-creatures, may be seen streets interlacing and crossing one another, winding in and out, growing wide in some places and so narrow in others that the inhabitants must walk in Indian file in order to pass each other. There are the "easy" paths already described, those traveled by the indolent and by persons addicted to the smaller vices and follies; there are the thorny, brier-tangled paths of deception and intrigue; the rough but wide thoroughfares of disobedience, uncontrolled temper, hatred, malice and revenge, all paved with sharp, jagged stones; and there is the road to crime.

It is of the last-named that I would speak. Scattered along this road may be found the varied devices of the shadow-fiends for luring mortals astray. Here a wine-glass, there a pack of cards, again a vile book or picture, and all along the way doors open into saloons, dance-halls and other dens from which strains of lively music may be heard issuing forth. Starting on this road from every conceivable one of the side streets, there is a continual procession of people, in captivity though they know it not, all passing onward to a more easily recognized bondage,—for this road ends within prison walls.

A strange scene was witnessed in a desolate home not long ago. In a white casket lay the still, marble-like form of a young wife and mother, slain by the hand of a husband who loved her devotedly. Around were grouped an aged, grief-stricken father and mother and two little bright-haired children; while in an adjoining room slept the youngest child, an infant of less than a year.

And the husband?

Wild with grief and horror at his own crime, of which he had not the slightest recollection, he was pacing up and down his prison cell with no prospect of release except the gallows, the fear of which was as nothing to him compared with his despair at the deed wrought while he was under the influence of drink.

But, you say, such cases, though sad and terrible, are not uncommon; why call this a strange scene?

Because the father and mother of the murdered one displayed an unusual spirit of toleration and even affection for her murderer. Their one hope now was to save him from the disgraceful death that awaited him. Though crushed by the sad fate of their only daughter, who had been the joy of their lives, they had only kind words for the one who had dealt the fatal blow.

"Whiskey did it," said the old man, with tears streaming from his eyes as he gazed into the motionless face, "John was always good to Katie when he was himself. A tenderer husband never lived. Why, he would not have harmed a hair of her head, if he had known what he was doing. It was not John who did this awful deed; it was whiskey. It would be terrible for the law to hold him guilty of murder!"

Yet the law does so hold him, and the family of children so soon to be doubly orphaned, will have a sad heritage of shame.

Drink is the immediate and fruitful cause of the great majority of crimes; this is a widely recognized fact. Yet thoughtful students of criminal conditions are inclined to go farther back and declare that even behind the drink lies another and deeper cause; that of wrong early training.

So says John L. Whitman, Superintendent of the Cook County Jail in Chicago. No man has had a better opportunity than he, to observe the causes and effects of crime; and no man is better qualified to speak on the wise and humane methods now being introduced largely by his efforts, to save the convicts from their worst selves, teach them respect for law, and make of them useful and trustworthy members of society. In quoting his words which follow, written especially for this book, I can therefore give my readers the most accurate as well as vivid idea of the slippery road which leads into crime both the ignorant hoodlums of the city slums and the thoughtless who have failed to profit by their better surroundings and advantages. Mr. Whitman says:

"It is easy, from one's fancy, to draw a picture of two young men, both now in the penitentiary, charged with, and probably guilty, of the same sort of crime and that is, murder, while a -robbery was being committed.

"One of these young men was brought up in the most vicious atmosphere and therefore had a very distorted idea of the difference between right and wrong.

"The other young man was brought up in a good family in one of the best parts of the city, where it could be easily supposed there were no evil influences; consequently, he had the best of advantages and had he seen fit to profit by them and by the advice given him, he perhaps would not now be serving time in the penitentiary on a charge of committing murder.

"Just imagine the different influences that were brought to bear upon these two young men to induce them to take part in such crime. The first young man was being fitted for a criminal career from infancy. The other was drawn into the commission of a crime after the age of reason had set in, but had not left its thorough impress on him; for he commenced by dissipation, then came thoughtlessness and reckless daring, encouraged in him by the idea that he was immune from the consequences of his rash acts, because of his station in life, his many friends and their social standing. So he continued in his wild career. However, he had no thought of murder or even crime in his heart; he just wanted to be a 'good fellow' and was unconsciously drifting along with the tide of sin until he found himself in the deep, swift current of debauchery, which carried him finally over the precipice of calamity into a prison cell.

"The first young man spoken of was one of that class that are early thrown upon their own resources. The street becomes their home, the den their school, the station house their college; such haunts become their world, from which they never emerge, except to exploit themselves in court, the bridewell or the reformatory.

"This particular young man had been a boot-black and had in other ways attempted to earn an honest living. He was not naturally a bad boy, as was afterwards shown by appealing to his true nature and getting from him original expressions on his views of the difference between right and wrong.

"His associations and environments were bad' and one night while aimlessly strolling the streets, he was accosted by two older men whom he had known in the neighborhood in which he 'hung out' and they said to him, 'Kid, don't you want to make a few plunks?' Of course, 'kid'-like, he said 'yes.' 'Now,' they said to him, 'don't be frightened, there will be no trouble; you just stand here and keep your eye peeled up and down the street and tip us off if the cop shows up and we will give you a piece of the money we get.' We are just going across the street here to get a little easy money.' The men went across the street, they entered the store, the unexpected happened, the proprietor of the store offered resistance and was shot, killed, the boy became frightened and ran away and so did the men. They were eventually caught, however, and all held for murder.

"Now, there was no thought of murder in that boy's heart. From my knowledge of him I doubt whether he would have had the nerve to handle a gun, let alone plan such a job, but in the eyes of the) law he was guilty. It would be but natural for a 'kid' to figure out in his own mind that he was innocent of crime. He would say, 'I had nothing to do with the actual commission of that crime. I could not help what those other fellows did, I was simply standing on the comer there and these men came along and said that they would give me a piece of money for staying there,' and we all know what an inducement a little piece of money is to such an urchin as he.

"Now, that lad was drawn into crime by the very life he was forced by his circumstances to live. The other young man was drawn into a like commission of a crime by a life he really knew better than to live, but had neglected the chances given him by more favorable circumstances to build his character strong enough to resist the temptations that surround the youths in our city. He, with his evil companions, committed his crime while drunk and thereby not only ruined his bright life and future prospects, but brought shame and disgrace upon his family and friends who love him."

From a talk with this leading penalogist I gathered, in short, that the chief causes of crime aside from drink are lack of right teaching while young, and in some cases, inattention to the best teachings; and that these conditions of moral ignorance and weakness, even more than deliberate vice, were the problems confronting those who had the care of the prisoners.

"In the desire to aid reformed prisoners on their release," I asked, "should society soon trust them with responsible positions? Should ex-convicts—the educated ones, I mean—be employed where they would have any financial responsibilities?"

"No, they should not," was the emphatic answer. "It would be no kindness, but rather, a dangerous temptation. The educated prisoners are the least to be trusted of all. They have proven morally weak, and the work given them must be such as will not tempt them to further falls."

"Then manual labor is practically the only class of employment open to them on their release?"

"Yes, it has been found the best way."

At this interview I secured the kind response of Mr. Whitman to the request that he would give my readers some of his views, methods, and experiences as to the reformation of the criminal. The following chapter is accordingly in his own words—the words, not of any mere sentimentalist, but of one who knows, and who has been tireless, ingenious, and remarkably successful in his efforts to help these weak ones who have fallen into the depths of the Shadow-World.

## The Boiling Kettle
### *The Sight of Hell*

Amos iv.—*"The days shall come when they shall lift you up on pikes, and what remains of you in boiling pots."* Look into this little prison. In the middle of it there is a boy, a young man. He is silent; despair is on him. He stands straight up. His eyes are burning like two burning coals. Two long flames come out of his ears. His breathing is difficult. Sometimes he opens his mouth, and breath of blazing fire rolls out of it. But listen! there is a sound just like that of a kettle boiling. Is it really a kettle which is boiling? No; then what is it? Hear what it is. The blood is boiling in the scalded veins of that boy. The brain is boiling and bubbling in his head. The marrow is boiling in his bones! Ask him, put the question to him, why is he thus tormented? His answer is, that when he was alive, his blood boiled to do very wicked things, and he did them, and it was for that he went to dancing-houses, public-houses and theatres. Ask him, does he think the punishment greater than he deserves? "No," he says, "my punishment is not greater than I deserve, it is just. I knew it not so well on earth, but I know now that it is just. There is a just and a terrible God. He is terrible to sinners in Hell—but He is just!"

# THE HOBBY FACTORY
### *Sermons by the Devil*

WHAT we here called the Hobby Factory represents one of the most remarkable branches of Satan's industries. It is a place where hobbies are manufactured for the use of such persons as can be persuaded to ride them. The following is given as an outline of an address delivered by Satan to the managers of this large factory.

"I am glad to meet with you on this occasion. It gives me great pleasure to look into the faces of those who have rendered such excellent service in my kingdom. I have called you together at this time to give you a few additional instructions relative to this particular branch of our work. It is quite evident that the use of Hobbies will never be out of date and in order for us to do more effective work we must improve on our present patterns, and keep adding new designs as rapidly as possible. We have found by past experience that we can reach certain people with a wooden horse quicker than with one of flesh."

"You deserve much praise for the manner in which you have induced many professing Christians to become radical and so narrow in their belief that they can easily confine themselves to riding one of these Hobbies. (Riding one idea to death.) I admit that you have some professing Christians that are hard to handle. They are charitable and do not allow themselves to live between high and narrow walls where the light can reach them at one angle only."

Note: The Devil does not like Christians whose hearts are open to the beams of truth shining from any direction. There is a type of broadmindedness that is well pleasing to Satan but not that kind in which the sincere heart is ever open to conviction.

As Satan continued to speak to the managers he put new earnestness in his voice:

"Whenever you can make a Hobby so attractive that an earnest Christian will confine himself to riding it instead of working in the great vineyard and sacrificing for Christ, you have won a good victory."

"In our work we meet with a certain class of earnest, devoted Christians on whom our teachings have no effect. They are temptation proof and Devil proof. What can we better do with such people than to get them to ride some Hobby. It is my experience that this method proves more effective than any other. If we can succeed in getting a good, well-balanced worker to run off on one line until he believes that his Hobby is the best of all, then it may happen that he will look down upon his brother as being his inferior in righteousness, just because he differs from him in opinion. The more we can kill charity among brethren, the more will the power of the church be crippled."

"There are many fault-finding church-members who can be persuaded to ride a Hobby. For these we ought to have some of special design, so that when they ride on them they will be rocked to sleep. When their eyes are once closed to the warfare of a Christian's life, they become an easy prey to any form of temptation that may come along."

"I rejoiced greatly as I looked over the wide field of our operations to see that we have in use several millions of Hobbies. The most of these are special doctrinal Hobbies. It is a pleasing spectacle to behold so many members of the church riding themselves to death on the lifeless horses - that have been manufactured right here in this wonderful building. You, my esteemed managers, must not think you are employed in any mean department of my service. If you do your work well, you are entitled to a rich reward. Even the most common branch of my work has its important features. In your labors you cannot be too ingenious, nor can you be too exact. Spare not the staining pot or the paint brush or the finishing materials. Your cares and your pains will find reward in good results. Just a few days ago I noticed that a man of considerable intellectual power, who might have made a good worker in the ranks of our enemies, was switched off on a tangent and it is very likely that the rest of his life will be spent in trying to prove that true baptism consists in being dipped backward into the water, and that any other form is null and void. This is quite a victory for our cause. Not because it is wrong to dip a person backward, but if we can get a person to believe that no other way is right, then he will regard many an earnest Christian as being out of harmony with Bible truths."

# 2

## Culture & Society

# Satan Preaches to a Society Woman
*Sermons by the Devil*

Subject: The disgrace of having children.

"What a blessed creature you are that fortune has smiled upon you so graciously. In the possession of so much wealth you have the noblest thing in life, for it is the means whereby everything else can he secured, and is indeed the secret of all true happiness. Money is power, and the absence of it causes dependence, misery and a long list of humiliating conditions."

"But of what use is your wealth if you do not allow it to bring you the greatest amount of happiness? If you would be true to society, and most sensible to yourself, you will see to it that in all your married life you will not be cursed with children. Let others, who are less fortunate than you, bear such burdens. You need all your time to fulfill your engagements, which are more numerous and more important by reason of your wealth. Disregard all this foolish talk about the inevitable yearning for motherhood, and hold your grand receptions and take your seasonable excursions and be ready at all times to enjoy the high and medium art of the stage."

"Why should your diamonds and your silks be idle for many months just for the purpose of having a child of your own, especially in these days when beautiful poodle dogs can be had for a mere song. Such creatures will not compel you to remain at home when you have a desire to go anywhere."

"If, in the hour of your weakness, you should crave for a cooing smile from a child of your own, or should wish to enjoy the thrill of two baby eyes looking into your own, you must remember that these are blind calls of nature to which your sensitive heart need not give heed. You must learn as early in life as possible to be your own mistress and let judgment instead of sentiment control you."

"You can comfort yourself with the thought that the God of earth and Heaven has destined you to fill one of the noblest places in the society of earth. The real truth of the whole matter is this: the bearing of children is an eternal disgrace, but in order to comfort the women who impose upon themselves this condition, the poets and philosophers have lauded the mother with her children. Surely you need not share in the disgrace since you are enlightened, and since you have abundant wealth to keep you employed profitably all the time."

## SOME THINGS SATAN FORGOT
## TO PUT INTO THIS SERMON

1. He forgot to tell this woman that the history of all ages proves that the disgrace rests upon the one in wedlock who refuses motherhood.

2. He forgot to tell her that if she heeded his doctrine her life would drift into an emptiness which nothing in the world could fill.

3. He also forgot to mention that all her wealth could not satisfy the instincts of human nature. The mother and the babe form a perfect pair, and each one needs the other to reach the highest happiness.

*The dark shadow of "Fashionable Society."*

## WOMAN'S DRESS — THE INDICATOR
## OF HER CHARACTER
### *Palaces of Sin*

IN this chapter we propose to take up the very delicate subject of woman's dress. However, there would be nothing "delicate" in regard to this subject, was it not for the fact that "Fashionable Society" makes it such.

When the female element of this "Fashionable Society" desires to dress in this unholy fashion they can not complain when decency rebels and points out to her the awfulness of her shame.

The reader may not know how society arrays herself when she attends these social functions, and I am quite sure that if the pure mothers and innocent daughters of this country were to look in upon some fashionable gathering, crowded by the devotees of frivolity, and behold those who claim to be ladies, attired, as they invariably are, in the low-neck dress and short sleeves, they would exclaim, "Oh! can it be possible that these women actually believe they are the modest creatures that God intended them to be."

I have beheld with my own eyes, young women and married ones as well, unblushingly come into the presence of men with their dresses cut so low in the back that two-thirds of their backs were exposed and these dresses were cut so low in the front that it is impossible for me to describe how absolutely indecent they were, but these women, without one blush of shame, would parade among the male sex without the slightest hesitancy. Not only would they unblushingly mingle with the male contingent of these society functions, but they would permit these men to waltz with them, which necessitated them placing their arms about her form, bringing them face to face with one another and nothing prevented him from gazing down upon her, and beholding her depravity.

The strange part of Society's dress is, that you never see women with bony arms wearing short sleeves; neither do you ever behold ladies who move in this class of society wearing these extremely low-cut dresses who have been deprived by nature of well-developed busts, as these "skinny" individuals invariably make "excuses" why they do not attire themselves in this fashion, which is indicative of harlotism.

I heard one lady say to another, "Oh! I always take cold so easy that I can not wear low-cut dresses" or "I have a birthmark between my shoulders or upon my bosom" and many other such excuses, but I have never in all of my association with this "Fashionable tribe" ever heard one of these devotees of fashion act the part of a pure woman and exclaim "I do not wear a low-cut dress because I believe that it is immoral."

When those women made these excuses for being decent, it was all a falsehood, as they did not want to acknowledge that nature had stinted them in the matter of plump arms and well-developed busts.

What can you expect of girls seventeen, eighteen or nineteen years old attending such places and gazing upon what they deem the leaders of society?

Can you expect these girls to be anything but immodest? Can you expect these girls after they become mothers to implant in their children's minds strict moral principles? No; it is an impossibility, as you can not impart knowledge you do not yourself possess.

These fashionable mothers set this immoral example before their girls when they are in pinafores, by dressing in this half-clad manner themselves, and when these girls grow up into womanhood they array themselves in the same fashion, for they had had their intellect stunted, as it were, from early childhood and never felt that pure womanly flush of shame rush to their brow at beholding such sights, as they were taught to believe that such was the "proper thing."

Oh! What a disgusting spectacle it is to see an old "fat-jawed" "society gusher" strutting around like an overfed goose (I beg your pardon, Mrs. Goose), wearing short sleeves and low-neck dress, and exposing herself to public gaze.

I have heard two or three times in my life some married lady who had not retained her girlish plumpness step up to one of these old, overfed "she devils" and remark, "Oh! Mrs. So and So, you are ten years older than I am and I can not account for your plumpness," and this old bunch of vanity would make a short "squat" which she intended for a bow, and say, "Oh! thank you," and would by way of explanation remark to this younger lady that "perhaps you do not know how to preserve your girlish appearance."

Of course, the other lady acknowledged that she was lacking that information, when this old, "perfumed half-century of sin" would tell her that "she had always brought her children up on the bottle, which was the secret of her retaining her girlish appearance."

I heard this conversation one evening while attending a "social" in the City of Brooklyn, NY. I, of course, was not expected to hear this. However, this old lady, with the short sleeves and low-cut dress, had attracted my attention early in the evening, and I could not keep my eyes off of her, not from her plumpness and girlish appearance, by any means, but she was one of the most ridiculous looking creatures that I had ever beheld, arrayed, as she was, as she actually looked more like a comic valentine than anything I could compare her to.

When she and this younger lady were talking, and when she made the remark about "bringing her children up on the bottle," I thought to myself, is it possible that society will go so far in her wickedness and in her desire to keep pace with her surroundings, that she will even sacrifice the health of her children that she may be pleasing in the eyes of the opposite sex? As it was plain to my mind that the only reason she wanted to retain her "girlish appearance" was to be noticed by the male sex of Society's followers.

This was the first time in all of my life that I ever heard any woman openly and unblushingly declare that she would willingly imperil the health and lives of her own children in order to appear "girlish" in the eyes of anyone, and especially a gang of lustful society degenerates.

Modesty is not an accomplishment, but it is an inborn gift from God, which every true woman has in her bosom until her corrupt associations destroy her modesty.

When you rob woman of her modesty you have robbed her of the greatest jewel, and when that jewel is gone she has but a short distance to travel before the "tongue of gossip" begins to "wag," and when this happens, her virtue is called into question, and when her virtue is destroyed she is an outcast among man.

Modesty, is woman's shield, and no woman can dress as "Fashionable society" demands and retain the respect of man.

The male sex may demand that she lay aside her "prejudices" as they are pleased to call it, but the demand is made in order that they may glut their lustful eyes at the expense of virtue.

I remember a bright eyed, sunny haired girl, about twenty years of age, from the State of Alabama, who visited her Uncle in Detroit, Michigan, about eighteen years ago. This girl had been raised upon a cotton plantation in Alabama, but who had been raised, thank God, by one of the South's dear "old fashioned" mothers. Oh! that we had a few more "old fashioned" mothers.

Jennie's Uncle was a man of affairs in Detroit, in fact he was what the world would call rich. He was a Southerner by birth but had married a Northern lady, and the daughter of a wealthy Banker in Detroit, who had been brought up to believe that it was all right to go into company half clad.

Her husband made a mild protest at first about her mode of dress, but he was soon silenced by the ironical "titter" of society, as they called him "A Southern Sunday School Boy," so it was not long until he ceased to offer any objections to his wife's immodesty. They never had any children born to bless their borne, so they were anxious to have Jennie Manley from Alabama visit them, as she was a beautiful girl with a most beautiful character. Jennie had always been used to plenty, that is plenty in a modest way, as her father was a cotton planter who was considered "well-to-do" by his neighbors.

Jennie's mother was loath to let her go to Detroit as she said she was afraid that the gay society her Uncle and Aunt moved in might put "queer ideas" into her head. However Jennie went, and returned to her father and mother without the taint of "fashionable society" upon her pure womanhood.

When she arrived at Detroit her Uncle and Aunt met her at the Depot that September evening, in their elegant carriage and drove her to their most elegant home in the fashionable part of Detroit, and Detroit you must remember, dear reader, is indeed a fashionable city.

Jennie was dressed in pure white with a pale blue ribbon deftly entwined about her girlish throat, which made her appear a typical country school girl. She was the picture of purity. When they arrived at her Uncle's home, this simple child of an honest Southern planter, gazed with wide mouthed wonder at the lavish splendor of her Uncle's mansion. She was a well bred girl and was above the average in intellect, but she could not but show her bewilderment at such grandeur.

Her aunt, about ten o'clock says, "Come, Jennie, I will show you to your room as I know you are tired after your long journey."

Jennie followed her up the broad marble stairs, which were a dream of splendor.

Her aunt led her into a room that was draped in oriental splendor, and says "Jennie dear, this shall be your room." Her aunt gazed upon this girlish figure which was as perfect as though it had been chiseled out of marble by the deft fingers of a classic workman. She gazed at her, clad in pure white, with that pale blue ribbon at her throat, and she declared to me afterwards that she did not believe her dress had cost over two dollars, but declared that Jennie was the most lovely woman she had ever beheld. Next morning after breakfast her Aunt said "Jennie, if you don't care I will take you to my dressmakers and have you a ball dress made." Methinks that the Angels in Heaven strained their ears to catch the reply, as a pure innocent country girl was having the first dart of the Devil cast at her by fashionable Society.

Jennie looked at her Aunt and replied, in a pure womanly manner, "I do not go to balls, therefore I need no ball dresses."

Many good resolves have been overcome by the fickle smile of society, so I imagine that even the angels were in doubt whether or not Jennie Manley would cling to her resolution.

Her Aunt says "Well we'll let the matter drop at present, but I think after a while you will change your mind."

The Aunt told me that she could not press Jennie that morning, for she felt that this pure child of the Southland was her master, but why, she could not tell.

Her Aunt informed Jennie that they were to give an entertainment that evening in her honor, and about four o'clock in the evening she remarked to Jennie "that they would drive up to a fashionable tailoress and see if they could not rent a suitable dress for Jennie to wear, for the occasion."

Again Jennie Manley straightened up with all her true Southern womanhood beaming forth from her deep blue eyes and says, "Aunt Mattie, if my own clothes, which my dear old mother and I have made, are not good enough for the people in Detroit, I'll take the train for Alabama this very evening, where I am respected as plain 'Jennie Manley,' and not for my clothes."

Oh! what womanhood. How many girls have we in this country like Jennie Manley?

Aunt Mattie, with tears in her eyes, reached out both hands and drew this girl to her bosom, and says "Oh! if you were my daughter I would be the proudest mother on earth."

Her Aunt told me in after years that this was the turning point of her life.

Jennie's feelings were hurt by her Aunt's requests to "get other clothes," but her Aunt soon gave her to understand that she was sorry she had offended her and assured her that as long as she stayed in Detroit she should wear what she pleased.

Evening came, and about nine o'clock carriages began to arrive, and the double parlors of this grand mansion were thrown open for the occasion, which was given in honor of Jennie Manley of Alabama.

I was on a business trip in Detroit, therefore received an invitation, as I was acquainted with the Standafords, but I had gone to Chicago that morning, and did not arrive at the Standaford mansion until all of the guests were there.

When I was ushered into the parlors of course this gang of "half dressed" women, and the tribe of "cut away coats" were there, and I was one more to add to this tribe. There were but two ladies in the audience who were not dressed in this immoral manner, and that was Jennie Manley and her Aunt. I was introduced to Jennie, and Oh, what a sweet child of nature she was. She reminded me of a meek violet surrounded by the rank and poisonous weeds of sin.

Wealth was there in all her brazenness. From the ears and throats of this gang of God's brazen creatures called women, flashed precious gems.

Young women were there whose marriage meant thousands to the poor wretch who dared tie himself for life to her, but around this pure and loveable girl from Alabama, clung the main attraction, as purity shone from her girlish face, and her smile was a tonic to famishing society, which knows nought but something artificial.

Supper was announced and served, and of course wine was there in abundance. When Jennie Manley's Aunt passed the vile stuff to her she said, "Jennie, here is a little that is half water, and I made it real sweet."

Jennie looked at her Aunt for a moment with her wondering big blue eyes, and said, "Aunt Mattie, it may be half water, but I do not care to even serve the Devil half way."

As though an electrical button had been touched that connected every man around that table, involuntarily, every one clapped his hands in honest approval, and I honestly believe the manhood of many had been aroused that had never been reached before.

When supper was over not a glass of wine had been touched, thus you see what determination and the will power of purity can do.

After supper the gentlemen retired to the "Smoking Room," while the ladies retired to the parlor, each lady endeavoring to pay homage to this country girl who had refused to obey the dictates of society, and who had with open hand smote the serpent of society without any apologies whatever.

Mrs. Standaford told me that while the ladies were together that evening one remarked to Jennie, "Why do you not wear low cut dresses Miss Manley, you have such a lovely form?"

Jennie looked her square in the face and says, "Why do you wear any dress at all?" This society lady says in reply. "Oh, that would be indecent." Jennie Manley remarked to this butterfly of fashion, "that is exactly why I do not wear low cut dresses."

Mrs. Standaford informed me that the evening was a very sultry one, as September you know generally is, but within a half hour from Jennie's stinging retort, every lady had complained of being "cool," and had thrown a cape or shawl over her nakedness.

Mrs. Standaford said, that the remarkable part of the thing was, that not one of these society ladies ever took offense at any of Jennie Manley's straightforward remarks.

Reader, here was a country girl who was inexperienced in what the word calls "knowledge" but she had the courage of her convictions, and kept God in sight at all times.

Several years afterwards, or after I had quit forever "Society's dissipations" I had a talk with Mrs. Standaford and she informed me that she knew of ten different society ladies, including herself, that never again wore a low cut dress, nor served wine upon their own tables, and each of them gave for their reason "that Jennie Manley from Alabama" had taught them a lesson they never forgot.

This pure, blue eyed Southern lass stayed in the City of Detroit several months, but she never forgot her early training, and never missed an opportunity to brand "frivolous society" with the hot iron of justice.

A Mr. Norton who was very wealthy became greatly infatuated with this sweet faced Southern girl, in fact, many "fell at her feet" and sought her "hand and heart," but Mr. Norton was naturally a gentle-

man until society spoiled him and dulled his manhood, and he endeavored to demonstrate to Jennie that he thoroughly coincided with her
in her hatred for the abominations of society, indeed he never missed
an opportunity to try to convince this girl that he had put away forever
everything pertaining thereto.

He was desperately in love with Jennie, but halted each time
that he thought of asking her to be his wife. Jennie never dreamed
that he worshipped her as he did, as she was under the impression
that he of course, was looking for some rich elegant lady, therefore
when he paid her many attentions she only believed it was done
through courtesy to her Uncle and Aunt. However, Jennie was soon
convinced differently, as Mr. Norton had gone to both her Uncle
and Aunt and laid bare the burden of his heart, and frankly told
them that he was desperately in love, but felt his unworthiness to ask
that pure country girl to become his wife, as he felt that he was so
much below her that it would be a disgrace to ask her to become the
wife of such a society renegade.

Mr. and Mrs. Standaford had known Mr. Norton from his youth,
and had always found him to be what "fashionable society" called
a gentleman. They also knew that he was very wealthy, consequently they were anxious to help the "match" along, so Mrs. Standaford
agreed to intercede, or plead his case with Jennie.

One chilly, dreary morning in November Mrs. Standaford called
Jennie into the library and drew her chair near the large open grate
which burned brightly, and says "Jennie, I have something I desire to
speak to you about, and the matter is vitally important to you."

Jennie like an innocent child as she was, turned her great blue eyes
to Mrs. Standaford, and says: "Oh, Aunt Mattie, you haven't received
any bad news from home have you?"

"No, no, my darling," replied her Aunt, "it is good news."

She began by saying "You know Mr. Norton is an awfully nice
young man, and he is one of the wealthiest young men in the city
of Detroit, which is saying a good deal, as we have many rich young
men here." She continued by saying "Mr. Norton called last evening
after you had retired and had a long talk with myself and your Uncle, and begged us to plead his case with you, therefore Jennie I have
come to you as an Agent for Mr. Norton to try to persuade you to
become his wife."

"To become his wife?" exclaimed Jennie Manley. "I marry that man? Never! I would rather have a mill-stone tied about my neck and be buried at the bottom of Lake Michigan than to be the wife of that man."

Her Aunt held her breath in amazement, as she did not believe this sweet faced Southern girl had so much spirit.

When Jennie had calmed down, Mrs. Standaford wanted to know her reason for branding Mr. Norton "as such a bad man."

"Plenty of reasons," replied Jennie. "He mingles with a class of men that would corrupt the morals of a saint, and with a class of women that are a disgrace to womankind."

"He allows his sisters to appear in public half clad, and drinks wine like the lowest of the earth, and if he does not know better, he is a fool, and if he does, he is a knave and a disgrace to his family, and no man that will brazenly drink wine before a lady, and permit his own sisters to unblushingly exhibit their nakedness in company can possibly make a true husband."

"Oh! Jennie, Jennie" exclaimed her Aunt, "you are too hard on us poor 'Society people,' however I can not but admire you, you dear bunch of, honesty."

"Then I suppose I shall tell Mr. Norton that you do not care to marry," remarked her Aunt.

"Tell him that I do not care to marry such as he," hotly retorted Jennie.

"Don't you ever intend to marry, Jennie?" asked her Aunt. "Yes, I do, and in May of next year, and the twenty-second day of May at that," replied Jennie.

"Well, well, if that don't beat my time," declared her Aunt. "You have been here nearly three months and never mentioned it to me before."

"What is your prospective husband like," inquired her Aunt Mattie.

"He is like the Greek Gods of old, only better," calmly replied Jennie.

"Oh, I would so much like to see him, haven't you his photograph?" asked her Aunt.

"I certainly have. Wait a moment until I go to my room and get it." Jennie returned with a cabinet sized photograph neatly wrapped up in pink tissue paper. She unwrapped it with reverential tenderness and handed it to her Aunt, saying as she did so, "there is the man who will be my loved and idolized husband on he twenty-second day of next May, if God spares both of us."

Mrs. Standaford took the photograph from Jennie and beheld the likeness of a smooth faced, broad shouldered, stalwart "son of toil" clad in the garb of a working man, in the act of rolling a bale of cotton on a pair of scales. He was a handsome open faced young fellow, and any one that ever had studied human nature knew that this Southern young man, who was not afraid of toil, was not only handsome but possessed the traits that mature into glorious manhood.

Jennie's Aunt was not slow in telling her that she considered him not only handsome but a noble looking fellow, which seemed to very much delight Jennie.

As the reader perhaps knows, the majority of wealthy people are always looking out for their children to marry some one possessing wealth, therefore it was very natural for her Aunt to ask "What prospects has your intended?"

"The grandest in the world" exclaimed Jennie, "as he has character and ambition and loves a girl that loves him, and if that is not enough prospect to enable any man on earth to clamber to the dizzy heights of success, then pray tell me what else is lacking?"

Early in January of the next year, Jennie Manley returned to her Southern home without taking with her a single taint of "Society's contamination" and on the twenty-second day of the following May, Jennie Manley became the happy wife of Robert Lee Overman, who is today a respected and honored man of the State of Alabama, and his wife the happy and contented wife of a Southern planter.

Reader the history of Jennie Manley and her victory over society is but one out of ten thousand, for where you find one girl that has the will powder to successfully combat the "She Dragons" and the "He Demons" of "Fashionable Society" you will find nine thousand, nine hundred and ninety-nine that will willingly, and without seemingly a single protest, glide down society's incline of shame, with such momentum that before they know it, they have wrecked their womanhood upon the shoals of society's degradation.

## The Sin of Wanting to be What We are not, and What We Cannot Afford to be.

How many homes have been wrecked by the inmates desiring to be what they are not, and longing to be just what their neighbors look to be.

The women, God bless them, are prone to be dissatisfied with their lot in life, as they behold the "finery" of their neighbors and become dissatisfied with their own clothes. They see the splendid carriages and matched teams their neighbors drive, and at once the Devil plants the seed of discontent in their hearts, and they either become envious or dissatisfied with their own surroundings, and dissatisfaction with your own surroundings is equivalent to being envious, and I can not think of a more miserable word in the English language than "envy."

You see your neighbors with their fine clothes, fine jewelry, fine furniture, fine horses and rigs, and you at once begin to compare your surroundings with theirs. You say, "I work just as hard as Mrs. So-and-So, and my children are just as smart and good looking as hers, but still I can't have all the elegant things that she and her children have."

You let your children know you are dissatisfied, and it is not long until you have them brooding over their "hard lot."

You plant the seed of "envy" in their hearts, and by your everlasting complaining and comparisons, you soon have a full grown weed of "envy" developed, to plague that child during the remainder of its days.

By your own acts you have made the life of your husband miserable, as he begins to notice that his children do not dress as well as those of his neighbors'.

What is the result? He either loses heart in his business, or makes a vow that his family shall dress as well as his neighbor's and makes one great effort and fails, and then with another resolve born of desperation he becomes a defaulter and robs his employer, or makes an assignment if he is in business for himself, as he has learned too late that the demands of his wife and children are too great for his once prosperous little business to sustain.

You do not stop to investigate and learn whether this family with their fine clothes and elegant "turn out" can afford it or not. You do not know that perhaps they "stint their stomachs" in order to appear in the eyes of their neighbors to be what they are not.

You do not know whether that family is happy with all of their fine equipage or not. You do not know how many sleepless nights that father has spent in racking his' brain to devise some way by which he may pay his obligations that his neighbors may not learn of his financial embarrassments.

It is a well known fact that some of the most magnificent oaks that adorn the forests have "wind-shaken" hearts, and so it is with at least one-half of the families who make a great show, their interior is all at fault.

Your wife and children have all the necessities of life that go to make home happy, as fine clothes, elegant carriages and high stepping horses do not make happiness.

Your children sit down to a table well laden with wholesome food, while perhaps the children of your neighbors who display their elegance and would impress you with their financial worth have a very meagre diet, for that mother who thinks more of impressing her neighbors with her great importance has to "cut expenses" somewhere in order to do so, therefore she begins at the table and goes right on down the line and "cuts expenses" everywhere, only so far as it would not affect outward appearances.

Does what your neighbors think of you add anything to what you actually are?

Does your neighbor dressing in elegance and sustaining a stable of fine horses and a beautiful carriage, work any hardship upon you?

"HONOR" is the rockribbed essential that you must have in order that you may know within your own heart that you are men and women, and no outward demonstration can convince you of this fact as this inborn knowledge must come by and through your own acts, therefore why need you "envy" that which your neighbor possesses and which does not add a hair's breadth to your stature or detract a particle from your manhood or womanhood.

Our miseries generally come from this innocent looking little word "envy" for we behold our neighbor with something that we do not possess, and we at once have a desire to have something "just as good" or better. In fact, we always try to go a little farther than our neighbor has gone, as we are not even satisfied to be his equal in appearance, but we want to impress him and our other neighbors that we are better, if anything. What is the result?

The result is simply this, that we tax our finances to a point where it becomes dangerous and it places us in "hot winter" as it were, to meet our obligations, as they fall due, and when we have once entered this silly practice, it is a great deal harder to stop it and "cut down expenses" than it would have been to have done without in the first place all of these things which does not add a moment's happiness to our lives nor does not raise us an inch in the estimation of our friends, for as soon as our friends and neighbors realize that we are going beyond what they consider our means, they at once consider us either extravagant or fools, therefore they lose their respect for us. You have not only lost the respect of your neighbors and friends who moved in the same circle that you once did, but you have caused those you patterned after to despise you, because they have to make another sacrifice to "outshine" you.

There are hundreds of mothers in this land who are satisfied with their dress until they see some one else with a better one, or at least one they think looks better, when at once they make themselves miserable by allowing this little word "envy" to assert itself. They are satisfied with their surroundings until they know of their neighbor's children having some garment that was bought in some "great city," when at once this poor old simple mother becomes dissatisfied with the clothes of her children, simply because they were bought at the "neighboring store."

What does this all lead to? Ah I nothing more nor less than a "Fashionable Society" right in the midst of the "common people," however, this "Fashionable Society" in the neighborhood is confined to the desire to "outshine" their neighbors in clothes, and has not yet reached the degrading stage of immorality, but we shade our eyes and look right down the line and we see these "country folks" establishing in a small way, a "Fashionable Society" within their midst that develops gradually into "Fashionable Society" of wealth, immorality and degradation.

Be it said to the ever-lasting honor and credit of the "common people" that you do not find so many envious individuals as you do among the wealthy. but the principle is as despicable among the poor as it is among the rich.

I knew a family in my boyhood who lived in the southern part of Indiana that was the "envy" of at least one-half of the neighbors and the other half endeavored to pattern after this family, as far as their clothes were concerned, however, be it said to the credit of this neighborhood they did not endeavor to follow their example as far as morals were concerned.

We will call this family by the name of Sharper for convenience sake. The father was a man who was very unscrupulous in regard to how he made his money, as everything was "grist" that came to his mill.

He owned a large farm and in addition to the revenues he derived from his farm he was interested in another business from which he made considerable money. The ambition of this family was to "outdress" and "outshine" all of their neighbors in every particular. They had no regard for God and his laws, therefore, of course, did not respect the laws of man to any great extent, and no further than was absolutely necessary to protect them from its clutches.

They had a number of both sons and daughters, and their ambition was to make their neighbors feel as small as possible when in their presence.

I am now speaking in a general way regarding this family, as one of the sons was several degrees higher in the scale of manhood than the majority of the children, however, he has never written his name exceedingly high on the "Tablet of Fame" in the profession which he follows.

This family had what could be termed a country mansion, elegantly furnished, fine horses and carriages without number.

Their father was a man of more than average intelligence, but he only used his intellect to get advantage of his fellow man and regarded his fellow man as only a "something" that he considered was his privilege to oppress, and he never missed an opportunity to oppress.

A man who does not respect the laws of God can not respect the laws of man, only so far as it is to his advantage to do so, therefore if he does not respect the laws of God and man, it is unreasonable to suppose that he possesses the finer feelings and nobler principles of man, consequently the reader will not be surprised to learn that he shamefully mistreated his own father, and a man or woman who will treat unkindly the father and mother who brought them into this world and cared for them when they could not care for themselves, is not deserving to be called "MAN."

From all outward indications one would suppose that this family with their elegance and seemingly every desire being granted, would live in happiness, but such was not the case, as there was a continual turmoil and dissatisfaction among the children, and you could expect nothing else, for when their father before them had turned from his door his old white-haired father, bent with years, upon the charity of his neighbors what could you expect of his children?

This family treated their neighbors as though they were created for their special benefit, consequently, of course, they were despised by the majority of the neighbors, however, these same neighbors would envy the Sharpers for their fine clothes and elegant "turn outs."

However, there came a day when prosperity seemed to turn to ashes of despair, and the black vulture of shame perched herself over this country mansion.

The father died. The children as well as the mother lawed among themselves, for the pittance the father had left, which was a very small amount, as his wonderful wealth in the imagination of the neighbors, had dwindled down to a very few thousand, and this amount was partially squandered in lawyers' fees and court costs by litigation among the children and mother.

Financial troubles could have been endured, but scandal after scandal attached itself to the members of this family, and today no family in that section is thought so little of as the one I write about, and no family in that neighborhood has as few followers.

The arrogance of their past actions only served as a hideous nightmare to haunt their present, and their future will be a desolate waste, strewn with bitter remembrances of the past.

This is the family that mothers once envied.

This is the family that caused discontent in the minds of the neighbors and their children. This is the family that fathers and mothers were envious of because they and their children could not wear as fine clothes and afford as fine "turnouts" as this Sharper family, but today the poorest family in that section holds up this Sharper family as a warning to their children and tells them of the arrogance that this family once possessed, but who has now been humbled in the dust, which is certain to follow in the wake of dishonest and unscrupulous transactions.

Contentment is more to be sought after than wealth, as the mind that is content with its surroundings, provided the individual has endeavored to make use of its God-given ability, is as near perfection as is possible in this life.

Ambition and contentment are two separate and distinct words. Ambition means a desire for greater things and contentment means, at ease, or a satisfied feeling, with present surroundings.

You may say that if you are ambitious that you can not be contented, but such is not the case, for if your ambition is a righteous ambition, it will be content and satisfied with your best efforts, and no man or woman can please God without putting forth their best efforts, which means satisfaction to your conscience, for whenever we fail to do our best, our conscience pricks us.

It would be just as reasonable for all of us to envy the great orator, the great singer, the great musician, or the great preacher, as it would for us to envy the man or woman who chances to wear better clothes than we do.

Do you suppose that the crow with his raven wings envies the tropical bird with its brilliant plumage? NEVER! The crow is content with the color of his dress!

Do you suppose that the eagle with his mighty scream which does not contain a single melodious note, envies the Nightingale, as she pours forth her beautiful melody? Never! That old eagle is proud of her harsh voice, and not one thought of envy does she bestow upon the sweet singer of the night.

Do you suppose that the nimble-footed deer of the forest envies the powerful ox his strength? Never I She is content with her meekness and agility.

Do you suppose the little star that glitters in the heavens looks with envy upon the moon in all of her glory? Never! The star has a mission to fill and does not for a moment envy the moon her magnificent splendor.

Contentment, then, is not only an indication of wisdom, but it is a duty that you owe God to be content with what your lot is, provided, however, that you have not, by some act of your own, made your lot a miserable one.

Contentment is the blessed assurance of having performed your duty, and both men and women know full well when they have righteously performed their duty, as that little thing, called "conscience" is nothing more nor less than the whisperings of an omnipotent God, which tells us when we have, or have not, performed that duty.

Oh! if the mothers and fathers of this land would banish from their minds every thought of covetousness, which is only another name for "envy," what happy homes we would have throughout the breadth and length of this land.

Let your neighbors wear silks if they like, but before you undertake to dress yourself and family in these expensive garments ask yourself, "Can I afford to do it?"

Wives and children, before you make your husbands and fathers miserable by your requests, first ask yourself, "Can our husbands and fathers afford it?"

Remember that while you are sitting in your little home envious of your neighbors' finery and their carriages and horses, that perhaps that awful weight of "debt" which is a nightmare and a hideous dream to any right thinking man or woman, may be weighing this family down and keeping their nose to the "grind stone" as it were, in order to make this outward appearance.

Ah! I would rather have the white winged dove of contentment to hover over my thatched roof and be able to look the world in the face and know that I owe no man a single penny, than to have the raiment of kings and queens and the equipage of oriental princes, than have my visions by day, and my dreams by night marred by that awful word "debt."

Reader, I hope this chapter does not fit you, but if it does, from this time forward make a resolve that never again will you be discontent with your surroundings, provided that you have done your best. Whenever you arrive at this conclusion your neighbors' children dressed in silks and satins will not disturb you in the least. There is an old saying that "Fine feathers make fine birds," but there was never a more erroneous statement uttered, as the feathers are no part of the bird.

Fine raiment may make fine looking ladies and gentlemen, but what is it that constitutes a lady or a gentleman? Is it their garments? If it is then we could dress up the most villainous criminal that ever went unhung, in broad cloth, with patent leather shoes, a silk hat, and place a two-caret diamond in his shirt front, and instead of having a criminal, whose hands are red with the blood of his fellow man, we would have a "gentleman."

If the garments that we wear make ladies and gentlemen, we could take the degraded harlot from the brothel, and dress her in silks and satin and immediately transform her into the noblest work of God "a pure woman."

When we learn that "envy" and covetousness" is the Devil's pet mode of leading mankind to the plains of misery, and that these two words—"envy" and "covetousness"—do not find lodgment in the minds of true men and women and in the minds of men and women of brains, then, and not until then will we realize that the most beautiful word in the

English language is "contentment."

## SATAN AND SENSUALITY
*Sermons by the Devil*

ONE day we met a man who had listened to many a sermon by Satan on the subject of the lower passions. He had been told that it was good for a man to be like the beast in his body, and in his mind to rise beyond the things, that are earthly. This teaching pleased the man, and consequently he tried to develop both sides of his nature so as to be well-balanced. The result was just the same as if you would throw a weight over the wings of a bird and then expect to see it fly away toward the blue of Heaven. The man had been told in one of Satan's sermons that nature called only for that which should be granted, and therefore that he should not deny himself by a constant restraint. It would be a long story if we were to tell what arguments Satan used to persuade this man to live the life of a libertine. He was confused by one fallacy after another, until the finer sense of his moral taste was perverted.

Speaking in general it is sadly true that Satan takes advantage of human inclinations, and strikes his telling blows at the weakest part of man's nature. As a result of this condition we find that there are many willing disciples who gladly render obedience to Satan's black sermons of Sensuality and Adultery. These sermons that seem to have a wizard influence are whispered in the ear of the soul, and blast the flower of purity more than cruel frost would blast a rose.

How sublime is the word of God in its portrayal of human nature. It mentions the flesh as one of the chiefest enemies, and teaches that he who conquers this foe is a real hero, and that he will receive a more glorious reward than kings bestow upon their favorites.

Look at one of the illustrious characters of the New Testament. He forged his way to the front through visible and invisible foes that threatened to overcome him. Paul proved his strength by his steadiness even when the thorn in the flesh was pricking out his patience. He lifts up his praises to God for this bitter means whereby he was enabled to scale mighty heights in his experience. The peculiar type of this conflict brought into exercise the strongest parts of his nature. The power by which he won this victory was the very force that made him master of his times.

*One cannot travel the by-path of adultery without falling into one or another of the traps of Satan.*

If Satan were honest he would confess that since he did not create man, therefore he does not know what is essential to his highest development. But God, who not only formed but sustains the human framework with its conscious soul connected, knows that the pathway to real achievement is rough, and covered with many a thorn. The man who is master of the flesh is a world-conqueror, and some day he will be 1uler over an empire more vast than any that earth ever knew.

Satan is not satisfied if a person takes one or two lessons in crime, or if he travel on the soul-deadening path of Sensuality, but he is constantly endeavoring to persuade people to travel on one or another of the degrading by-paths that lead off from Sensuality. One of the most famous of these by-paths is the one called Adultery. Satan or one of his agents is ever standing at the junction of these two roads and putting forth every effort to induce those who have gone into Sensuality to travel off into Adultery.

As you look at the picture you can see how careful Satan is to place the traps of Adultery behind a cliff of rocks, so that they who travel on the path of Sensuality cannot see the destruction into which they are so liable to fall. The temptations of the enemy are manifold to persuade people into this calamity, and if one sets his foot upon the path of Adultery there are always grinning imps enough, as you see in the picture hiding behind the rocks, to pull the trap door, so that he may suddenly stumble into the abyss of ruin.

It should be clearly understood that the Devil is the sole owner of the many paths that lead off from Sensuality. He has one path called Fornication, upon which many are induced to travel. To such he offers a beverage of obscenity which so deadens their sensibility that they stumble on in crime with a thoughtlessness that is appalling.

Another by-path of Sensuality is called Concupiscence, which leads off into a vile park. There are other by-paths to correspond to every shade of sensual sin. Thousands of demons are employed all along this black district, sapping the life-blood of the millions, and destroying the souls of all who allow themselves to become slaves of the lower nature by following the dictates of fleshy lusts.

We would sound a word of warning: Do not travel on the general path of Sensuality, which is in the territory of the Devil. If you keep off of this path you will not be led into any one of the terrible places such as are indicated in the picture heretofore mentioned.

The only reward that Satan offers to any one who enters upon Adultery is pollution and defilement in sugar-coated form. This, when taken, is so blackening that its stain cannot be erased from the soul by any power except Almighty God, and then only at the earnest supplication of the one defiled.

# 3
## WEALTH & BUSINESS

## SATAN'S BUSINESS ADVICE
*Sermons by the Devil*

"IF a man enter upon some kind of business to gain a livelihood for himself and family, it is his duty to so conduct his affairs as to make it pay. A business man has the right to perform certain tricks which in themselves are perfectly proper, even though the world or the church may condemn them. People who are not in business do not fully understand how many intricate problems there are to solve and how many little trials there are to bear."

"To state the whole matter briefly, I would say that a soft, tender conscience and a wide-awake business man make poor companions. If you wish to succeed in business you must observe the following rules:

1. "Learn to prevaricate without lying."

"Prevarication is pleasing to the people and without it you will have a disappointed class of customers. It is certain that people expect you to shade the truth a little, or they would not ask such foolish questions most every time they come to purchase. If you are selling an article worth one dollar, the customer is pleased if you tell him that it is worth two dollars. He is not particular whether you are telling the truth or not. All he cares about is that he can tell his friends that he is wearing an article worth two dollars."

2. "Become expert in the use of 'bluff.'"

"Bluff is the most modern way of lying without violating the law.

83

In purchasing goods you can so talk that the manufacturer will believe that you can buy cheaper elsewhere. If you put these bluffs at him in a modern style, it may compel him to yield, and perchance you may clear several dollars in your deal."

3. "You must learn to make heavy profits wherever you can."

"Your policy should be to get for an article what you can and not what is right. You will find that before you are through with your business career that you need all the margins that it is possible for you to make. You should, as quickly as possible, have a reserve fund so as to be prepared for any emergency."

4. "You must learn the art of adulteration and make use of this knowledge to best advantage."

5. "In order to avoid competition, form a monopoly if possible."

"This is the great secret of large business success. You could not expect to become a power in the business world so long as you are hampered with a lot of small trade centers, each one doing a business similar to your own. The motto of the age is: Combine interests, either drown out or buy out the small firms, and get a full control of the line of business which you represent. Do not allow the cries of a weak reformer or a nervous public to make you believe that this is wrong. You must stick to the policy that anything is right that you can do and escape from the civil law."

## A REPLY TO SATAN'S BUSINESS ADVICE.

When one studies the methods of Satan in the business world he is strongly impressed with the numberless ways in which dishonesty and deception are practiced under a cloak of righteousness. Satan says with a show of boldness that "A tender conscience and a wide-awake business man make poor companions." This is a false statement and is only believed by the man or woman whose conscience has already been warped. In business or in any other vocation the only way to reach real success is by the way of honesty. It is true that a rascal may endure for a season, and heap unto himself great wealth and thus appear to enjoy the highest success in life, but all this will prove in the end a curse to him.

The majority of those who fail in business are not the conscientious men, but those who have had their ears open, more or less, to Satan's business advice. We have a sure word of prophecy that rings out the following note: "As the partridge sitteth on her eggs, and hatcheth them not; so he that getteth riches, and not by right, shall leave them in the midst of his days, and at his end shall be a fool." Jer. 17-11.

Satan gives a few rules which he claims must be observed if one would wish to reach success in business. The first one is "Learn to prevaricate without lying." This is only another way of saying, learn to tell a falsehood without lying. The only safe way in business is to tell the truth. By doing so, you may occasionally lose a sale or a customer but your loss will be your gain. Your truthful qualities will lift you gradually to a substantial throne of honor.

"Bluff" is the refuge of the hypocrite. There are times when one has a right to pass off a pleasantry or an innocent joke, but whenever anything of this kind is used to cover real facts in a business deal, then it changes to the color of a lie.

In the third advice given by Satan there is a peculiar mingling of truth and error and it is in such kinds of arguments that Satan ripens the mind for greater error. It is not always right to get what you can for a commodity. There is a difference between might and right and there are thousands who take advantage of situations especially in monopolizing, and by getting what they can they get considerably more than what is right or just. There is no rule in business so precious as the Golden Rule.

One need not resort to unlawful adulteration or to any other type of illegal or unrighteous actions. This is the Devil's pathway of success down to eternal destruction. If you are honest and righteous to your full ability, you will enjoy the peace of a clear conscience through all your business years, and in the evening of life you will have precious meditations and the sweetest reflections. And most glorious of all when your eyes close to this life, Eternity will dawn with a full radiance of immortal glory and you will be receiving your reward forever.

## ON THE RICH AND POOR
*Hell Before Death*

AMONG the many causes of unrest among the workingmen is the manner in which certain rich people use their wealth, and the spirit which they manifest toward the poor; also the attitude of certain corporations toward their employees in times of strikes and during other kinds of disturbances. Among the rich there are many who have used, and are still using their wealth in a very commendable manner. These exceptional cases are the bright lights along the path of financial frenzy. The man who realizes his responsibility, and studies to use his wealth in the best possible manner, is a mighty moral force, and is ever giving rebuke to the selfish, miserly men of wealth whose sole ambition is to grasp and accumulate at any cost.

The rich man should recognize his many obligations, and, if he wishes to please God, he must not forget that he is a steward, and is held responsible for the manner in which he uses his wealth, and all the other powers at his command. This law is so simple that it needs no line of proof. The fact of human responsibility to God is one of the greatest realities of life. The poor man must also give an account of his stewardship in finances, influence, opportunity, ability and every other quality of the body and soul. If money is one's greatest power, then money is also one's greatest opportunity to do good, and he should not use it to oppress individuals, or impose burdens on society, which will all come to light in the final day of reckoning. There is no truth more firmly established than that man must give an account of his deeds in the body, at the final judgment.

We have personally known in our time a few men of moderate wealth, who keenly realized their responsibility to God. Their daily prayers breathed out the request to the Infinite One for guidance in the handling of their money. Suppose that all the corporations and money kings of our country yielded the fruits of such a spirit, would there then be any cause for labor uprisings? No general movement would be known, for our Social System, defective as it is under the cloud of private ownership and competition, would then render to every man a fuller product of his labor.

It needs no argument to prove that the spirit of the great majority of our rich men and our rich corporations is just the opposite from what it ought to be. The heartless rich are using their vast possessions as absolutely their own; they seem to care not for God, for man or Satan. A true photograph of this class reveals a picture of indifference, heartlessness, foolishness, and fashionable robbery.

## FOOLISHNESS OF THE RICH.

When we speak of the foolishness of the rich, we refer to the bold extravagances that have made the blood of the poverty-stricken classes run fire. When we hear tales of more money being spent by a wealthy woman on a poodle dog than a workingman spends on a whole family, we are disgusted; when we hear of thousands of dollars being wasted to gratify the morbid appetite of a man of wealth, we are shocked; when we hear of wild frivolity at a reckless cost, we are more than ever reminded of our own hopelessness, if we ever fall into the hands of such reckless rulers.

Think of the women who spend millions to gratify their pride and love of fashion, in the very midst of swarming poverty and discontent. The artist who wishes to draw a picture of selfishness, can find no better model than the man or woman who is making a frantic effort to spend as much money on himself or herself as possible, while he turns a deaf ear to the cries of the suffering world.

There is a law of Scripture, "Unto whomsoever much is given, of him shall much be required." There are too many of the wealthy who interpret this word "much" to mean much extravagance, fashion, much of the overbearing spirit, much tantalizing of the poor. Dr. G. V. Reichel very forcibly says:—"The privileged class must set a better example of living before the circumscribed classes can be uplifted. It is only too appallingly true that the power of wealth in its oppression of the poor, is, in many instances, not short of murderous. Hence we witness a change of opinion concerning the privileged class; and the much vaunted ease, the unjustifiable indolence, and the ofttime unquestioned worthlessness, so characteristic of it, had disenchanted the vision of wealth, and excited among the poor a bitterness of hate that grows ominous."

We are not alarmists, but we wish to say in the line of history, that the Reign of Terror came like a thunder roar after the gathering storm of ages, and the conditions existing now in our country indicate that unless radical changes occur, there will come some calamity of which no one can now make an adequate prophecy.

# HOW THE RICH EVADE THE LAW
*Hell Before Death*

"THE sons of rich men who spend their time gambling and consorting with harlots, having had their gambling dens in Chicago temporarily closed, chartered a ship and went out on the lake where the racing reports were wirelessly sent them and there gambled. This is known to all the people; the papers prate of it; the gamblers and the disreputables gloat over it—and what is done about it? Nothing. They are rich and the rich cannot be punished for crime. The officers say there is no law to punish them! But how quickly would a law be found to punish them if they were poor! If there were no law they would be punished without law."

"Indictments have been returned by the federal grand jury against the teamsters in Chicago on charges of violating 'police morals' and 'trade morals.' When labor undertakes to get better conditions for itself 'it is a conspiracy.' When a man like Bigelow filches a couple millions, it is a 'breach of trust.' Broken heads and jail sentences for the working class, and banquets and trips to Europe for the bankers who swindle confiding depositors."

It is very difficult for the laboring man to get laws passed i in his favor. Recently the Legislature of Colorado refused to enact an eight-hour-day law after the people had sanctioned and demanded it by ballot. This was the voice of the working masses and it was not heeded by the lawmaking body. When corporations can so influence a State Legislature, is it not true that public government is at an end, and revolution is at hand? Nothing is so much the cause of the present uneasiness and the general disrespect for law as this partiality in its administration.

"Government should also protect the poor man's property against the rich man's fraud, as well as the rich man's property against the poor man's stealing. There are selfish and lawless men in each class that will get their neighbor's goods without an equivalent if they can. * * * If there is any difference, the rich banker, who steals the wages of the poor committed to his keeping, is a worse rogue than the sneak thief who steals the banker's overcoat, yet the last is stealing and the first is embezzlement, and if the embezzlement is managed with considerable skill, the criminal may still be in good society. Such false distinction should be done away with and all the thieves whether rich or poor be upon an equality."

Another source of uneasiness is the manner in which honest people are fleeced out of their money by misrepresentations and by common agreement amongst captains of finance. The great revelation along this line by Thomas W. Lawson in "Everybody's Magazine" will not be forgotten by the American people for a long time to come. Let us quote one of his general comments on the Wall Street Speculations:—

"The truth is that in high finance all civilized amenities have long been suspended. The black flag is to-day the Wall Street standard. Thuggery and assassination are so much the rule that nowadays all parties to a business transaction wear armor and carry stilettos. Property rights are vested in Power; the sole license to have, is strength to hold; to covet another man's railway or factory is, if you be the stronger, full warrant and charter to its possession. In the pursuit of 'made dollars' greed and cunning lead the pack; kindliness, fair dealing, and truth have lost the scent. To-day the penal code is Wall Street's bible; its priest, the corporation lawyer; conscience is a fear of legal consequences; the sole crime, being caught; talent and character are best proved by a large bank account; to err is to fail; continued success in speculation and a few years' immunity from retributive justice constitute a reputation for virtue and stability that finds its highest justification as a handy asset behind a bond issue.

"It is the deplorable fact that in carrying through the great deals that have marked the last few years, it has become a habit for men to lie, cheat, bribe, and commit perjury, and there is no more condemnation of such practices among those who are to-day the representatives of finance in America than there was in earlier times for the close-fisted driver of a hard but honest bargain."

Should anyone consider that this "word picture" of Wall Street is overdrawn, he has the privilege of investigating for himself, providing he has the necessary time and ability to do so. We feel safe in saying that any competent investigator will have his eyes more than opened after he has thoroughly completed his work as a detective. It required such a man like Lawson, who lived on both sides of the Wall Street fence, to give a full word picture of the black crimes committed in the dark in the name of decency, and even Christianity. These stealthy criminals escape the penalty of the law by secrecy, bluff, arrogance and bribery. The middle class and lower class of people are fleeced out of their money by all kinds of promising schemes, and, whenever the guilt has been properly placed, the offender is punished very lightly if punished at all, and the sufferer has no way to regain his lost money.

The day is not far distant when the large army of speculators will be called upon to do their share of honest work. It will then be seen how much of the Wall Street machinery is really necessary to the successful maintenance of our government.

# 4
## CHILDREN

## IN SATAN'S SCHOOL ROOMS
### *The Devil of Today*

WE had now come to the part of the building which contained the School of Modern Methods.

Unseen, we entered the class-rooms where teachers provided by His Satanic Majesty were busy instructing their pupils.

"Seest thou how carefully the work is done?" inquired the Angel.

"Yes," said I, "and each pupil seems anxious to catch every word of the instructor."

There were classes in deceit, in gambling, lying, thieving, murder, money-getting by up-to-date methods, and other diabolical arts; and I learned that each student was expected not only to benefit himself, but to disseminate what he learned in so subtle a manner as to seduce those of the world among whom he mingled.

There was one class much larger than any of the others, at which I wondered. The teacher was engaged in his work as we entered the room, and we heard his words.

"You are to be shrewd and plausible. Hold back for no consideration, except that of losing the prize for which you aim.

The end always justifies the means. Tell the lie boldly, and in all misrepresentations look men in the face with calm eyes, lest they detect your motives. Do as the world does, and never waste any time in debating whether a thing is right or wrong. You are in it to win, and win you will, if you modernize your methods of approaching men."

"What class is this?" I asked.

"This is Satan's class of modern business methods, and the students here are from various representative professions. They are eager 'to get rich quick,' by the latest methods of the Devil," was the reply.

"Do not regard any one as a brother," the instructor continued. "Disguise your motives and strike home. What though you do cause another to lose; his loss will be your gain, and if a lie can win you the best of the bargain, use it and you will be considered the most up-to-date man on the street, and no one will be the wiser as to the secret of your success. Don't be conscientious in your dealings, for thereby many have remained poor, and crept along at the slow pace of self-denial all their lives. Live for this world."

These words were eagerly taken down in note-books with which each pupil was provided, and as we left the room, the students were in the act of applauding one of the striking sentences of this diabolic address.

## Satan on Child Training
### *Sermons by the Devil*

"There is certainly a wrong opinion prevailing among some people regarding the early training of a child. Even though the world is several thousand years old, yet people will not learn by the follies of the past. A child is the greatest bundle of possibilities in the world, and we cannot expect the best results to follow if the mind of the child is spoilt during the first seven years of its existence."

"If you notice the policy which is pursued by some parents and guardians, you would infer that the child must be filled with all kinds of moral lectures and religious nonsense, until he groans under the terrible weight. To compel a child against its will to go to Sunday School or church before it is seven years old, is about the best way to ruin its mind for life."

"One of the first requisites of a good mental training is to teach self-dependence, and, as quickly as possible, get the individual to see things for himself. If it be your fond desire to have the child go to religious services, let the influence of a good example draw him, and not the severity of the rod or the sharp lectures from the lips."

"Allow a child to enjoy its natural liberty so that its expansion may be full and free. There is plenty of time for the weightier things, if the child's life is spared. The first seven years should be free from toil and restraint of any kind, except what the child may choose. In this manner the child will soon regard work as a pleasure. Think of the terrible effect it must have on a child's mind to put it into early slavery under a rod of fear. In this manner it is taught that life is a burden and that liberty, if it is to be enjoyed, must be a stolen pleasure."

"It would be better to keep a child out of Sunday School until he is seven years of age, and then allow him to go if he chooses. Constantly tell him, by your actions and your words, that religion is not intended to give a man greater liberty than he would otherwise enjoy, but on the contrary it often tends to narrow a man down to a set of hard rules. If religion were properly taught, it would have a wholesome effect upon the human race, but taught as it is in many places, it throws a dark gloom over what ought to be the brightest walks of life."

"Regarding the home instruction, a parent ought to be especially careful to impress upon the mind of a child nothing concerning the unseen world. Take the first seven years to teach a child concerning the things which he can see, hear and touch. Let him become thoroughly acquainted with the world of sense and sight before you attempt to launch him into that mystical realm of the unseen. You must not attempt too much during one period of life. Attend to one thing well and see to it that genuine development is reached. If this advice is adopted you will find, at the end of seven years, a child with a fine body, healthy in all of its parts which will be a mighty foundation upon which a wise instructor can nobly build."

"The great majority of people in this age of the world are determined to follow in the rut, and because their predecessors practiced the cramming method in the education of children, so they imagine that they must do likewise. What the world needs at this time is a number of reformers who will have the boldness and courage to teach the benefits of the method I have just advanced. Then, under the new teaching, the body will not be sacrificed for the sake of the mind, but the mind will begin to expand in the proper realm at the proper time. Then we shall see the beginning of the brightest era since the creation of the world. Until then let each one strive to fulfill the law as here advanced, and the great reward is sure to come."

## A Brief Reply to the Preceding Sermon on Training Children

If the Devil would tell the truth, he would teach much differently on this subject than he has expressed in this preceding sermon. Satan knows that the first seven years of a child's life is very important in the shaping of its character. He also knows that if a child is not placed under control during this first period, that it will be almost impossible to control it afterward.

The teaching of Satan regarding the development of the body to the exclusion of the spiritual training during the first years of a child's life, is senseless and not worthy of attention. We believe that the body should be developed without impairing the mental faculties, and also that the soul should have a healthy growth without interfering with the natural body. There is no better time in life to leave deep impressions on a child's mind, than during the first part of its existence. Then you can teach it concerning the existence of a supreme being, and of the immortal life.

No child should be allowed to do as it pleases unless it pleases to do right. A boy or girl must early learn to be submissive to the will of another. If this is not learned its life will be more dangerous than a ship without an anchor on a stormy sea. Satan knows very well that if a child is not submissive to its parents, or to the true God, that he himself will gain control over its life.

Satan uses some beautiful expressions to show the outcome of his teachings, if they were observed. All this promise of a happy end is a wicked phantom, and is as untrue as Satan himself. He borrowed a picture of the Millennial Dawn and used it totally out of its connection.

The most distressing feature of the situation is this: there are many people who follow the teachings of Satan in full or in part. We hope that they will turn a deaf ear to the enemy and give their children the training that will bring the highest possible results.

# 5
## MISCELLANY

## HARMLESSNESS OF SIN
### AN OBJECT SERMON BY SATAN
*Sermons by the Devil*

ONCE upon a time, Satan addressed an audience of worldly-minded Christians. He had prepared himself with objects by which to make a deeper impression of what he wished to teach. In one hand he held a branch of a fruit tree, that had been partly eaten by worms, but which contained good clusters of fruit. In the other hand, he held a beautiful branch on which the mark of the worm pest could not be seen, but this branch had no fruit.

"I appear to you this day to teach you the truth regarding the results of sin. You have heard it said that all sin is harmful. But I have come to tell you differently. A little sin becomes stimulating and works to a good end. Look at this fruit-bearing branch which I hold in my hand. It has been attacked by little worms until their marks of destruction are plainly visible all over it. Yet this has only stimulated the life of the branch, so that it has borne fruit abundantly. The best fruit in life is borne in sin, therefore I would urge you not to be afraid of certain small sins. You can see that the other branch has been free from the enemy's blight, and yet it has borne nothing but leaves."

"This fruitless branch is a fair sample of those people who want to be so pious and goody goody in life. They make a beautiful showing, but bear no fruit. As you walk along the pathway of life, you will notice that the best results come, not only from pure illumination, but by the that a weight was removed so that I could breathe more freely.

The stairway was a steep and winding one, ending at the very top of the building, in a small tower. Here we entered an odd little round-shaped room furnished in gray, with two windows overlooking the mountain side. But my guide did not go to the windows. Instead, he led me to a seat in front of a large gray curtain.

"These pictures that I must show you are not pleasant ones," he said, "but they are, alas! true to life. In fact they are alive; only what you see is a reflection of the real occurrences, exactly as in a mirror. We could see the real ones themselves from the window if it were not so dark. As it is, the reflection will answer quite as well. Now I will draw aside the curtain. Look!"

I gazed as my guide lifted the curtain. The picture was marvel-lously lifelike. A light shone from it—or through it, I could hardly tell which,—making the human figures look as if about to step from the canvas. Not even Delorme's painting of "The Blacksmith" could be called more realistic.

The picture showed a mother seated in a plainly but cozily fur-nished room with her two children playing by her side. The room was that of a country home, with few luxuries but much substantial com-fort. The woman was sewing; both she and the little ones, a boy and a girl, were happy and healthy looking, and the picture would have been a pleasing one but for two ugly shadow-forms that lurked in one corner of the cottage room, unseen by its inmates, and apparently whispering together while pointing maliciously towards the children.

The picture suddenly faded, and another took its place.

This was a street scene in a great city at night. The youth and maiden who were the central figures were clearly the two children of the first scene, grown older. An open door of a saloon was near, into which the boy was being smilingly invited by a young man, while a flashily dressed woman approached the girl. What had become of the mother, I did not know, but the shadow creatures lurked in the corner.

The third picture was that of the interior of a dance hall. Flimsily dressed girls with painted faces were dancing, while the rude jests or meaning glances of their evil-looking companions seemed to cause in some the wildest merriment, though to a few of the younger and more innocent they brought evident distress and consternation. Here, as in mingling of the lower light with the higher. It is a case of two opposites flashing together to form the vital spark. Only as the soul is touched by sin can it reach its highest level. This does not necessarily mean that sin must predominate. One must learn how to live and serve a noble purpose, and at the same time entertain a little sin in his heart. I trust that you will leave this room to-day with broader views of life, and that you will not despise all sin because certain ones have such a black color."

## SATAN IS IN AN UGLY MOOD
### *The Devil of Today*

A BAND of fiends came rushing up the path, and as they beheld Satan they halted and waited for him to speak.

"Where were you when Artful was in the grounds?" he demanded of them.

"Guarding the castle," they replied.

"A nice lot of guards you are!" said their master in derision. "Why did you not help Artful to accomplish his purpose of self-destruction?"

"The Angel persuaded him from it before we could reach him," ventured one of the band in reply.

"If we could have gotten hold of him first, the capture of his soul would have been an easy matter," added another.

"You must have been frightened by the Angel," Satan declared. "Why were you afraid of her?"

"There was a strange light around her," one confessed, "and before we could recover from our fright, she had saved him from the deed."

"I thought so," said Satan, with increasing rage; "you are a lot of silly cowards."

## COMMON TRAPS
*The Devil's Doings*

ON my second trip to the Under-World I had a nearer view of the shadow-creatures. My errand led me straight to the old fortress which I saw was their headquarters. Grim and forbidding it loomed up in the flickering light; for the volcano was more quiet this time at the moment of my arrival, and the flames shot up only to subside and leave the city in a twilight which might almost be called more gloomy than absolute darkness. A gigantic spider's web was stretched across the doorway of the huge old building.

"Has no one entered here lately?" I asked the guide, pausing as he brushed aside the web for us to pass through.

"Not in this door," he replied. "The shadow-creatures enter through the low arch you see yonder," pointing to an opening with an inscription over it in some foreign tongue. "But this other door is the visitors' entrance, and has not been used for a long time. Most people content themselves with a surface examination of the shadows' work; they do not look deeper."

"Then if the shadows go in through the low arch," I said, "where do they work after they are inside? Are any of them in there now?"

"Yes, indeed," was the answer. "The main office is half full of them now, and here come some more."

The shadows were faint because the light was so dim, and 1 could not see them plainly at the first glance. But I saw enough that was horrible in their snake-like movements to cause cold shivers to run down my spine, even while the perspiration stood in drops on my forehead. The sense of utter loathing which these creatures inspire is more than can be described.

"Do not fear them," said my guide, reassuringly. "They will not be allowed to harm you, or even to see you. They have other business. Terrible business, too! Revolting beyond words, for any one to witness! But you can do little to stop it until you understand; hence I am going to let you see what this work is. Come with me."

I followed the guide up a narrow stair, my courage and my curiosity returning as I went. I had need of both, to carry me through this nightmare of experience. Even though I knew I was quite safe, I felt relieved as we left the shadow creatures behind for the time being. I felt the first and second pictures, the shadow fiends were plainly to be seen, and they looked particularly well pleased.

Next came a picture of a gambling den where the youth of the other pictures sat with flushed, excited face playing cards with several men, most of them much older. Glasses of some kind of liquor stood on the table, and it needed not the exultant look on the shadow faces to tell me that a dispute had arisen, perhaps to end only in murder and overwhelming disgrace.

The pictures followed one another in rapid succession. A drunken millionaire plunging madly along in his automobile and crushing the life out of a woman who could not get out of the path of the wild racer; a drunken husband locking his wife outdoors on a stormy winter night; a drunken father sending a bullet through the head of his fourteen-months-old baby; these were only samples of the frightful list. As for the sequels to the dance hall picture, they were found in the wretched, wild-eyed outcasts who sought oblivion by plunging from a bridge into the deep waters of the river; and in the madhouses full of shrieking victims; and in the Potter's Field. No words can describe the horrors of those pictures as the work of saloon, dance hall and gambling den was slowly unfolded from the seemingly trivial beginnings to the tragic end.

"Take me away!" I cried with a shudder, at last, turning to my guide. "I can look no longer. Let us leave this dreadful place. How can such things be?"

"Come, then," was the reply. "But he sure it is all true. The temptations are so insidious that the young do not realize where they are drifting. Let us go down and listen for a few moments to the kind of arguments used by the shadow fiends in the beginning, to persuade the young folks that these things are harmless."

I rose from my gray cushioned chair just as the curtain was allowed to fall on the scene of a heartbroken mother raving in a sudden and hopeless insanity over a murdered son, killed in a saloon,— and as I passed the window I saw the volcanic fires leap up with renewed fierceness till the country roundabout seemed indulging in a wild dance of fiendish glee at the sufferings of mortals. I would be glad indeed to forget that night; but I cannot. It is burned on my memory by a fire that is still lighting up those worst of all scenes in the Under-World.

I scarcely knew where I was going, but followed my guide below till a door was reached opening into a room broad at one end but quite narrow at the other. At the opposite end of the room, as we entered the door, was the one thing of supreme interest and importance in this world of strangeness,—for there, blazing with its own heat, and seldom free from use, was the Red Telephone.

The shadow creatures began to come in. This was more than I could endure, after the horrors I had already seen. I must have turned white with repugnance, for my guide, in pity, led me to a chair facing away from the telephone, where I could not see the messengers who came to it, though their words were quite distinct. The voices themselves were not unpleasant. They had been trained too carefully for their work, to express in tone the true nature of the speakers.

"Hello!" called one, a moment after ringing the bell. "Is that Harry Stevenson? Well, this is Guy Goodfellow. I want you to promise to come down to Carter's to-night. There'll be a lot of splendid fellows there that I want to introduce you to, and a jolly good time for everyone.

"What's that? You don't believe you can come?

"Why not? You never do go to Carter's? Oh, bosh! It's time yon did, then. Why, man alive, there's no harm in it.

"You don't drink? That's all right; of course; you needn't if you don't want to. Just come down and see the fellows, that's all. We'll have a game or two of billiards, and go home early. Come, don't refuse."

"You'll come just for a little while? Yes? Good for you! I knew you were the right stuff. We'll have no end of fun, for we're going to start a club down there—just a social club, no harm in that, you know. We'll want you for one of the officers. Be sure to be on hand. All right; good-by."

"That is the *beginning,*" commented my guide, quietly, as the voice ceased. "Carter's is one of the traps of the Under-World, a saloon. Harry will go, intending to drink nothing but soda, and to go home early. But it will not stop there. Very soon he will take 'just one glass' of something, with the others, to be sociable, and then he will take more than one; the evenings will grow long until by degrees they stretch far into the night. Anxious, careworn parents, an ungovernable appetite, a ruined career, all await him as the result of that telephone message. Yes,—this is the beginning. The end—is such as you saw in the pictures upstairs!"

Another messenger had taken the first one's place. In a few minutes by a similar course of reasoning, a young man was persuaded to enter another of the Under- World's traps—a gambling den. He was assured there was "no harm in a social game of cards," and reminded that many reputable people played. But the trap was sprung, nevertheless.

The third message was in a foreign language, and I could not translate it. My guide kindly acted as interpreter, and I learned that this most fiendish of all plans was that of the "White Slave Trade" carried on notoriously in Philadelphia, and probably no less in other cities,—the enticing of young girls into dens of infamy from which there is no escape.

"Only young girls of from twelve to sixteen years," explained my guide, "are desired. Older women know too much to be easily managed by the den keeper. The young girls are inveigled into these places on one pretense or another by paid agents of the 'White Slave Syndicate.' As a rule none of them can speak English. They are told that they must submit because such is the custom of the new country to which they have come. They are not allowed any privileges. They are very scantily supplied with clothing. They are not given anything in the line of wearing apparel in which they could appear in the street, even if the door of the den were not kept locked and bolted. They are not allowed even a small percentage on the profits of their own infamy. A more revolting, diabolical, devilish thing than the 'White Slave Trade' of the 'City of Brotherly Love' could not be conceived in the head of any devil incarnate even if that brain were kept on the rack for a thousand years. It is enough to make every decent, self-respecting man blush with shame that such a thing is possible under the Stars and Stripes."

One would think, surely, that in this visit I must have exhausted all the possibilities of the Under-World! But, no; there were other traps in reserve. This was winter. In the summer the shadow-fiends are no less busy, as perhaps we may see.

Only two more messages were to come, on this occasion.

"Hello, Jack!" called a voice at the phone. "Come around to the theater with me to-night. I've got an extra ticket for you. Just drop everything for once and come. I tell you it's a hot one—this vaudeville on Clarkson street. It'd be a shame to miss it. Lots of pretty girls—

regular daisies. Music is the best ever, and the dancing and jokes are wide awake, you bet. You'll laugh fit to split your sides. Rob and Sam are coming, too, and we'll make a party of it. You be round the corner of Blake street, and I'll meet you there. Don't let on; the folks might kick. Gee! but we'll have a hot old time! You'll be there sure? All right, good-by."

My guide made no comment on this message. None was necessary, I knew what it meant—this cheap vaudeville performance, with its coarse jokes, indecent rather than humorous, and the costumes, music, dancing, and all, of just the kind calculated to blunt the finer sensibilities and lower if not destroy the manliness of these bright, eager young fellows just starting in life. I was about to protest, when still another voice, a crafty, seductive one, was heard urging Miss Innocent to go that night to a dance hall, "just to see what it is like. There's no harm," the voice went on.

But suddenly there was a sound as of a rushing wind, and I turned, forgetting my dislike in my curiosity to see what was happening at the phone.

There seemed to be a momentary struggle between two shadows; then the newcomer succeeded in pushing the other aside and reaching the phone herself. For this shadow was—or had once been — a woman, or rather a young girl. There was little semblance of youth or beauty now!

"No! no! no!" she fairly shrieked, into the telephone. "Don't go! I went once, and it was once too often! Do they tell you there's no harm in it? There is harm—there is the blackness of horror and death in it! You never will come out the same girl that you were when you went in! There's ruin and death in the dance hall—I know it too well, for I was caught in that trap and the disgrace was more than I could bear and live! Take warning, take warning from me—for I am Mabel Wright!"

This startling message from the girl who took poison and ended her earthly life in a dance hall but a short time before, had a disturbing effect on the nerves of the shadows—if shadows can be said to have nerves. They flocked into the room from every direction, with threatening looks and gestures, toward the only one among them who had rebelled at the laws of the Under-World.

I had but one more glimpse of this one who called herself Mabel Wright. I could not be sure, the group of angry shadows surrounded her so closely, but I thought I saw a change pass over her; a change for the better, leaving her face less wretched and almost peaceful. But the sight rapidly faded from my view, for I suddenly awoke, and this, my second visit to the Under-World, was over.

## SATAN'S VIEWS ON SWEARING

Spoken to an Educated Young Man, Whose Conscience was Troubled on Account of his Profanity.
*Sermons by the Devil*

"IT is impossible to draw the line between swearing and not swearing. There are so many words necessary to give strength to our sentences that he who wishes to be forceful in his speech makes a serious blunder in barring out all manner of by-words. How wisely the good teacher of Palestine said that it was not that which came out of a man that defiled him, but that which went into him. So if the heart is right, one need not worry so much about the words that pass from the mouth."

"The many harmless words used in swearing only add flavor to your conversation and give you an opportunity of expressing the exact shade of your feelings. No one would think of becoming shocked at the common types of profanity if it were not for the prejudice which is quite popular against swearing. When charity once reaches that standard of excellence for which all good people crave, then there will no longer be this deep-seated prejudice against the salt, pepper and spice of our language."

"Constantly remember, my young friend, that you are a free creature, and that you can do as you please. But on account of the civil law try to avoid the rank types of profanity lest some fool should have you arrested."

"Have you ever noticed that the men who swear are usually men of big hearts and kind dispositions. If there is need of charity in the community, three chances to one, the man who swears will be the first one to give substantial help, while the pious church people will possibly not know anything about the needy case until it is too late."

We can see by the foregoing remarks that Satan totally ignores the teaching of the Bible, such as is found in the following passages:

Ex. 20:7, "Thou shalt not take the name of the Lord thy God in vain, for the Lord will not hold him guiltless that taketh his name in vain."

Lev. 19:12, "Ye shall not swear by my name falsely, neither shalt thou profane the name of thy God."

Zech. 5:3, "Every one that sweareth shall be cut off."

Col. 3:8, "Put off all these, blasphemy and filthy communication out of your mouth."

When profanity is so expressly forbidden in the greatest book in the world, and is also contrary to the civil law, then no one ought to listen to the wicked teaching of Satan on this subject.

It is easily understood that if Satan had his own way every mouth would flow with black curses. He knows very well that when a person can be persuaded to take the name of God in vain that he is unfit to worship the same God in spirit and in truth. Or to put the matter more plainly he is lending his influence to the service of Satan.

Satan has a peculiar way of quoting Scripture. He stops short in the middle of a verse or reverses the order of the thought just as he sees proper to carry out his low purpose. When he makes reference to the "Good teacher of Palestine" he quotes the passage in a manner altogether misleading. It is a hundred times better to never look at the Bible than to use it for such purposes.

Satan tells a black falsehood regarding the character of the men who swear. Swearing has never made anybody charitable or kind and it is strange that anybody should tolerate such views. The world has received its greatest blessings from the people who respect and worship God and who could not take His name in vain under any circumstances. The world's march of progress has been along the line of the pure in heart and pure in words. In the language of another let us say that "The man who swears does ten things at once."

1. He breaks the command of God. 2. He violates the law of the land. 3. He transgresses the rules of good manners. 4. He outrages decency. 5. He insults good people. 6. He profanes sacred things. 7. He shows bad bringing up. 8. He dishonors his parents. 9. He does what he is ashamed of. 10. He does what he will regret.

# 6

## FINAL WORDS

## THE DEVIL'S LAST SONG
*Sermons by the Devil*

THE time is coming when this young world of ours will be old and decrepit with age, when the proudest monuments of human glory will have crumbled to dust. The empire of sin shall then fall to pieces and its king shall be chained in the bottomless pit, far off from the gates of Heaven. Can we not imagine that when this time shall have come, Satan will sing his bitter song somewhat after the following lines:

"Long ago I planned in my passing pride,
That to-day I would reign as king.
But where is my kingdom, where is my crown?
Is the bitter song that I sing."

"What joy have I won through my evil designs?
What peace in my soul-wrecking plan?
I hoped to conquer both Heaven and Hell
But have won nothing more than man."

"I can see above, o'er the bridgeless gulf,
The glorified Heaven-lit strand,
My chains make me feel the double disgrace
As I crouch 'neath the Infinite Hand."

"Where are my princes, my legions of dupes,
And the millions of souls I won?

My pains and my chains are greater by far
Because of the deeds I have done."

"All my plans and my schemes in a thousand ways,
Like bubbles are blown out of sight,
My fancies and hopes like a passing dream
Are covered by shadows of night."
"Come on, all ye dupes, ye millions of men,
Who heeded my wishes like fools,
Take your share for aye of the galling chains,
Under Him who in triumph rules?"

"You have lived and died for my noble cause,
Your souls are eternally marred,
You shall see no more than glimpses of light
Of Heaven from which you are barred."

"Then fling all your hopes, my friends, to the winds,
As the echo of sadness replies,
You will feel henceforth the deeper degrees,
Of the Hell which beneath us lies."

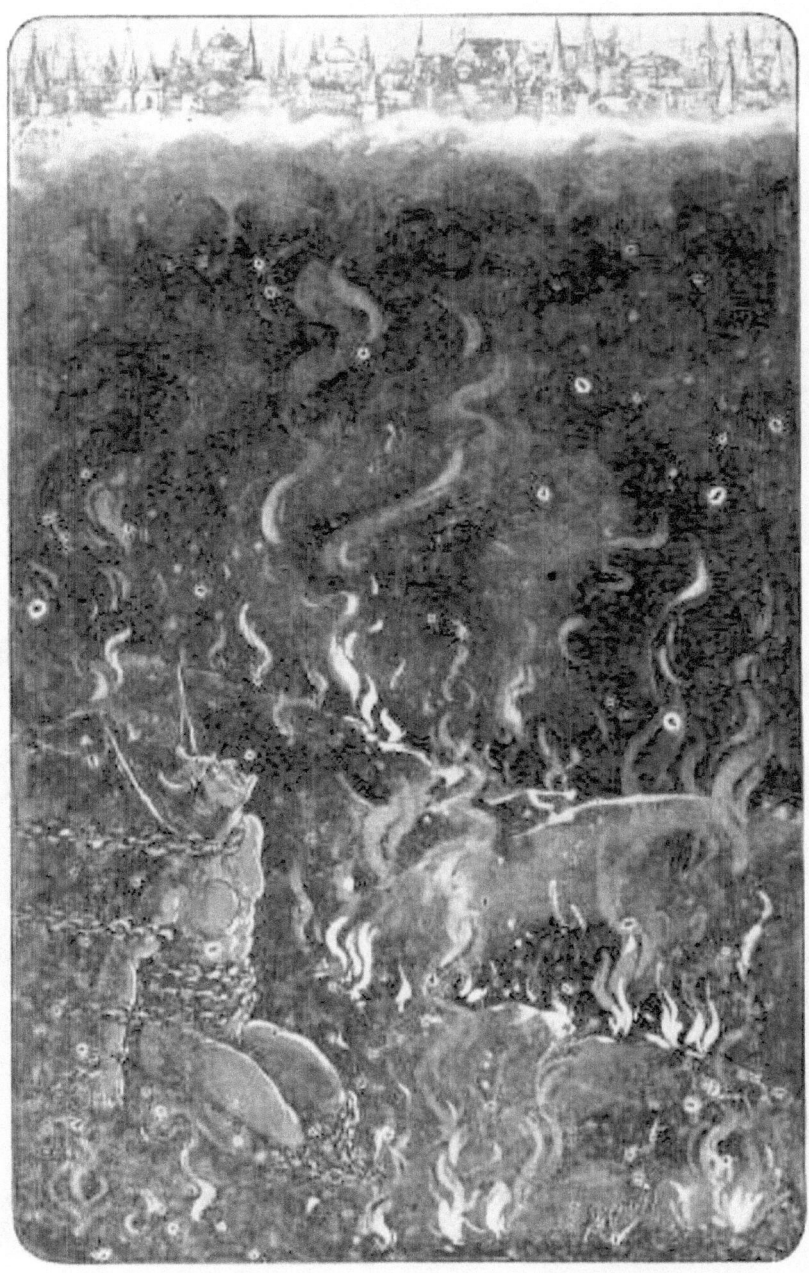

*At last Satan will be bound in the bottomless pit, whence he can look over the bridgeless gulf to the far-off City of Light.*

www.ingramcontent.com/pod-product-compliance
Lightning Source LLC
Chambersburg PA
CBHW020825150626
46554CB00018B/2473